CLEP* PRINCIPLES OF MARKETING

Anindya Chatterjee, Ph.D.
Slippery Rock University
Slippery Rock, PA

James R. Ogden, Ph.D.
Kutztown University,
Kutztown, PA

James E. Finch, Ph.D.
University of Wisconsin
La Crosse, WI

Denise T. Ogden, Ph.D.
Penn State Lehigh Valley
Reading/Fogelsville, PA

Research & Education Association
Visit our website at: www.rea.com/studycenter

Research & Education Association
61 Ethel Road West
Piscataway, New Jersey 08854
E-mail: info@rea.com

CLEP Principles of Marketing with Online Practice Exams

Published 2014
Copyright © 2013 by Research & Education Association, Inc.
Prior editions copyright © 2006, 2005, 2003, 2001, 1999, 1996 by
Research & Education Association, Inc. All rights reserved. No part
of this book may be reproduced in any form without permission of the
publisher.

Printed in the United States of America

Library of Congress Control Number 2012954088

ISBN-13: 978-0-7386-1095-5
ISBN-10: 0-7386-1095-X

Cover image: © istockphoto.com/JamesBrey

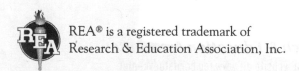

CONTENTS

ABOUT OUR AUTHORS

James Finch is the director of the M.B.A. program at the University of Wisconsin–La Crosse. He has also served the university as interim associate dean of the College of Business Administration and as a graduate faculty member. Dr. Finch holds a Ph.D. from Ohio State University.

James Ogden is the chair of the Department of Marketing at Kutztown University in Kutztown, Pennsylvania. He has formerly taught at Cedar Creek College, Central Michigan University, and the University of Northern Colorado, among others. Dr. Ogden received his Ph.D. in College Student Personnel Administration from the University of Northern Colorado, and received his M.S. in Marketing from Colorado State University.

Denise Ogden is an assistant professor in Marketing/Business Administration at Penn State Lehigh Valley in Reading/Fogelsville, Pennsylvania. She has also taught at Allentown College/DeSales University and Cedar Crest College. Dr. Ogden holds a Ph.D. in Business Administration from Temple University.

Anindya Chatterjee is an associate professor of Marketing at Slippery Rock University in Slippery Rock, Pennsylvania. He has previously taught at Temple University, from which he received a Ph.D. in Marketing.

ABOUT RESEARCH & EDUCATION ASSOCIATION

Founded in 1959, Research & Education Association (REA) is dedicated to publishing the finest and most effective educational materials— including study guides and test preps—for students in middle school, high school, college, graduate school, and beyond.

Today, REA's wide-ranging catalog is a leading resource for teachers, students, and professionals. Visit *www.rea.com* to see a complete listing of all our titles.

ACKNOWLEDGMENTS

We would like to thank Dr. Scott Miller for technically editing the manuscript; Pam Weston, Publisher, for setting the quality standards for production integrity and managing the publication to completion; John Paul Cording, Vice President, Technology, for coordinating the design and development of the REA Study Center; Larry B. Kling, Vice President, Editorial, for his supervision of revisions and overall direction; Diane Goldschmidt and Michael Reynolds, Managing Editors, for coordinating development of this edition; Transcend Creative Services for typesetting this edition; and Weymouth Design and Christine Saul, Senior Graphic Designer, for designing our cover.

PART I

Passing the CLEP Principles of Marketing Exam

PASSING THE CLEP PRINCIPLES OF MARKETING EXAM

Congratulations! You're joining the millions of people who have discovered the value and educational advantage offered by the College Board's College-Level Examination Program, or CLEP. This test prep covers everything you need to know about the CLEP Principles of Marketing exam, and will help you earn the college credit you deserve while reducing your tuition costs.

GETTING STARTED

There are many different ways to prepare for a CLEP exam. What's best for you depends on how much time you have to study and how comfortable you are with the subject matter. To score your highest, you need a system that can be customized to fit you: your schedule, your learning style, and your current level of knowledge.

This book, and the online tools that come with it, allow you to create a personalized study plan through three simple steps: assessment of your knowledge, targeted review of exam content, and reinforcement in the areas where you need the most help.

Let's get started and see how this system works.

Test Yourself and Get Feedback	Assess your strengths and weaknesses. The score report from your online diagnostic exam gives you a fast way to pinpoint what you already know and where you need to spend more time studying.
Review with the Book	Armed with your diagnostic score report, review the parts of the book where you're weak and study the answer explanations for the test questions you answered incorrectly.
Ensure You're Ready for Test Day	After you've finished reviewing with the book, take our full-length practice tests. Review your score reports and re-study any topics you missed. We give you two full-length practice tests to ensure you're confident and ready for test day.

THE REA STUDY CENTER

The best way to personalize your study plan is to get feedback on what you know and what you don't know. At the online REA Study Center, you can access two types of assessment: a diagnostic exam and full-length practice exams. Each of these tools provides true-to-format questions and delivers a detailed score report that follows the topics set by the College Board.

Diagnostic Exam

Before you begin your review with the book, take the online diagnostic exam. Use your score report to help evaluate your overall understanding of the subject, so you can focus your study on the topics where you need the most review.

Full-Length Practice Exams

These practice tests give you the most complete picture of your strengths and weaknesses. After you've finished reviewing with the book, test what you've learned by taking the first of the two online practice exams. Review your score report, then go back and study any topics you missed. Take the second practice test to ensure you have mastered the material and are ready for test day.

If you're studying and don't have Internet access, you can take the printed tests in the book. These are the same practice tests offered at the REA Study Center, but without the added benefits of timed testing conditions and diagnostic score reports. Because the actual exam is Internet-based, we recommend you take at least one practice test online to simulate test-day conditions.

AN OVERVIEW OF THE EXAM

The CLEP Principles of Marketing exam consists of approximately 100 multiple-choice questions, each with five possible answer choices, to be answered in 90 minutes.

The exam covers the material one would find in an introductory college-level marketing course. This type of course is commonly titled Basic Marketing, Introduction to Marketing, Fundamentals of Marketing, Marketing, or Marketing Principles. Such a course—and thus the exam itself—covers the role of marketing in society and within a firm, understanding consumer and organizational markets, marketing strategy planning, marketing institutions, the marketing mix, as well as topics such as international marketing, ethics, marketing research, services, and not-for-profit marketing. The CLEP candidate is also expected to have a basic knowledge of the economic/demographic, social/cultural, political/legal and technological trends that undergird a competent understanding of marketing.

The approximate breakdown of topics is as follows:

8–13%   The **role of marketing in society**, including ethics, non-profit marketing and international marketing.

17–24%   The **role of marketing in a firm**, including the marketing concept, marketing planning and strategy, marketing research, marketing information system, and marketing environment.

22–27%   **Target marketing**, including consumer behavior, and marketing segmentation, positioning, and business-to-business markets.

40–50%   The **marketing mix**, including product and service management, branding, pricing policies, distribution channels and logistics, marketing communications/promotion, and e-commerce.

ALL ABOUT THE CLEP PROGRAM

What is the CLEP?

CLEP is the most widely accepted credit-by-examination program in North America. The CLEP program's 33 exams span five subject areas. The exams assess the material commonly required in an introductory-level college course. Examinees can earn from three to twelve credits at more than 2,900 colleges and universities in the U.S. and Canada. For a complete list of the CLEP subject examinations offered, visit the College Board website: *www.collegeboard.org/clep*.

Who takes CLEP exams?

CLEP exams are typically taken by people who have acquired knowledge outside the classroom and who wish to bypass certain college courses and earn college credit. The CLEP program is designed to reward examinees for learning—no matter where or how that knowledge was acquired.

Although most CLEP examinees are adults returning to college, many graduating high school seniors, enrolled college students, military personnel, veterans, and international students take CLEP exams to earn college credit or to demonstrate their ability to perform at the college level. There are no prerequisites, such as age or educational status, for taking CLEP examinations. However, because policies on granting credits vary among colleges, you should contact the particular institution from which you wish to receive CLEP credit.

How is my CLEP score determined?

Your CLEP score is based on two calculations. First, your CLEP raw score is figured; this is just the total number of test items you answer correctly. After the test is administered, your raw score is converted to a scaled score through a process called *equating*. Equating adjusts for minor variations in difficulty across test forms and among test items, and ensures that your score accurately represents your performance on the exam regardless of when or where you take it, or on how well others perform on the same test form.

Your scaled score is the number your college will use to determine if you've performed well enough to earn college credit. Scaled scores for the CLEP exams are delivered on a 20-80 scale. Institutions can set their own scores for granting college credit, but a good passing estimate (based on recommendations from the American Council on Education) is generally a scaled score of 50, which usually requires getting roughly 66% of the questions correct.

For more information on scoring, contact the institution where you wish to be awarded the credit.

Who administers the exam?

CLEP exams are developed by the College Board, administered by Educational Testing Service (ETS), and involve the assistance of educators from throughout the United States. The test development process is designed and implemented to ensure that the content and difficulty level of the test are appropriate.

When and where is the exam given?

CLEP exams are administered year-round at more than 1,200 test centers in the United States and can be arranged for candidates abroad on request. To find the test center nearest you and to register for the exam, contact the CLEP Program:

CLEP Services
P.O. Box 6600
Princeton, NJ 08541-6600
Phone: (800) 257-9558 (8 A.M. to 6 P.M. ET)
Fax: (610) 628-3726
Website: *www.collegeboard.org/clep*

CLEP EXAMS MIGRATING TO iBT

To improve the testing experience for both institutions and test-takers, the College Board's CLEP Program is transitioning its 33 exams from the eCBT platform to an Internet-based testing (iBT) platform. By spring 2014, all CLEP test-takers will be able to register for exams and manage their personal account information through the My Account feature on the CLEP website. This new feature simplifies the registration process and automatically downloads all pertinent information about the test session from My Account, making for a more streamlined check-in.

OPTIONS FOR MILITARY PERSONNEL AND VETERANS

CLEP exams are available free of charge to eligible military personnel and eligible civilian employees. All the CLEP exams are available at test centers on college campuses and military bases. Contact your Educational Services Officer or Navy College Education Specialist for more information. Visit the DANTES or College Board websites for details about CLEP opportunities for military personnel.

Eligible U.S. veterans can claim reimbursement for CLEP exams and administration fees pursuant to provisions of the Veterans Benefits Improvement Act of 2004. For details on eligibility and submitting a claim for reimbursement, visit the U.S. Department of Veterans Affairs website at *www.gibill.va.gov.*

CLEP can be used in conjunction with the Post-9/11 GI Bill, which applies to veterans returning from the Iraq and Afghanistan theaters of operation. Because the GI Bill provides tuition for up to 36 months, earning college credits with CLEP exams expedites academic progress and degree completion within the funded timeframe.

SSD ACCOMMODATIONS FOR CANDIDATES WITH DISABILITIES

Many test candidates qualify for extra time to take the CLEP exams, but you must make these arrangements in advance. For information, contact:

College Board Services for Students with Disabilities (SSD)
P.O. Box 8060
Mt. Vernon, IL 62864-0060
Phone: (609) 771-7137 (Monday through Friday, 8 A.M. to 6 P.M. ET)
TTY: (609) 882-4118
Fax: (866) 360-0114
Website: *http://student.collegeboard.org/services-for-students-with-disabilities*
E-mail: ssd@info.collegeboard.org

6-WEEK STUDY PLAN

Although our study plan is designed to be used in the six weeks before your exam, it can be condensed to three weeks by combining each two-week period into one.

Be sure to set aside enough time—at least two hours each day—to study. The more time you spend studying, the more prepared and relaxed you will feel on the day of the exam.

Week	Activity
1	Take the Diagnostic Exam at the online REA Study Center. Your score report will identify topics where you need the most review.
2–4	Study the review, focusing on the topics you missed (or were unsure of) on the Diagnostic Exam.
5	Take Practice Test 1 at the REA Study Center. Review your score report and re-study any topics you missed.
6	Take Practice Test 2 at the REA Study Center to see how much your score has improved. If you still got a few questions wrong, go back to the review and study the topics you missed.

TEST-TAKING TIPS

Know the format of the test. CLEP Internet-based tests are fixed-length tests. This makes them similar to the paper-and-pencil type of exam because you have the flexibility to go back and review your work in each section.

Learn the test structure, the time allotted for each section of the test, and the directions for each section. By learning this, you will know what is expected of you on test day, and you'll relieve your test anxiety.

Read all the questions—completely. Make sure you understand each question before looking for the right answer. Reread the question if it doesn't make sense.

Read all of the answers to a question. Just because you think you found the correct response right away, do not assume that it's the best answer. The last answer choice might be the correct answer.

Work quickly and steadily. You will have 90 minutes to answer 100 questions, so work quickly and steadily. Taking the timed practice tests online will help you learn how to budget your time.

Use the process of elimination. Stumped by a question? Don't make a random guess. Eliminate as many of the answer choices as possible. By eliminating just two answer choices, you give yourself a better chance of getting the item correct, since there will only be three choices left from which to make your guess. Remember, your score is based only on the number of questions you answer correctly.

Don't waste time! Don't spend too much time on any one question. Remember, your time is limited and pacing yourself is very important. Work on the easier questions first. Skip the difficult questions and go back to them if you have the time.

Look for clues to answers in other questions. If you skip a question you don't know the answer to, you might find a clue to the answer elsewhere on the test.

Acquaint yourself with the computer screen. Familiarize yourself with the CLEP computer screen beforehand by logging on to the College Board website. Waiting until test day to see what it looks like in the pretest tutorial risks injecting needless anxiety into your testing experience. Also, familiarizing yourself with the directions and format of the exam will save you valuable time on the day of the actual test.

Be sure that your answer registers before you go to the next item. Look at the screen to see that your mouse-click causes the pointer to darken the proper oval. If your answer doesn't register, you won't get credit for that question.

THE DAY OF THE EXAM

On test day, you should wake up early (after a good night's rest, of course) and have breakfast. Dress comfortably, so you are not distracted by being too hot or too cold while taking the test. (Note that "hoodies" are not allowed.) Arrive at the test center early. This will allow you to collect your thoughts and relax before the test, and it will also spare you the anxiety that comes with being late.

Before you leave for the test center, make sure you have your admission form and another form of identification, which must contain a recent photograph, your name, and signature (i.e., driver's license, student identification card, or current alien registration card). You may wear a watch. However, you may not wear one that makes noise, because it may disturb the other test-takers. No cell phones, dictionaries, textbooks, notebooks, briefcases, or packages will be permitted, and drinking, smoking, and eating are prohibited.

Good luck on the CLEP Principles of Marketing exam!

PART II

Principles of
Marketing Review

PRINCIPLES OF MARKETING REVIEW

The following Principles of Marketing review is divided into nine sections, as follows:

    1:   **The Marketing Environment**

    2:   **Marketing Research**

    3:   **Target Markets**

    4:   **Product Planning and Management**

    5:   **Distribution Systems**

    6:   **Wholesaling and Retailing**

    7:   **Promotional Strategy**

    8:   **Pricing Policies and Strategies**

    9:   **Special Topics in Marketing**

By thoroughly studying this course review, you will be well-prepared for the material on the CLEP Principles of Marketing exam.

1: THE MARKETING ENVIRONMENT

MARKETING AND MARKETS

Marketing is the process of planning and executing the development, pricing, promotion, and distribution of goods and services to achieve organizational goals. Marketing directs the flow of products within an economy from producer to consumer by anticipating and satisfying the wants and needs of the market through the exchange process.

A **Market** is made up of all the people or organizations who want or need a product and have the willingness and ability to buy.

Products may be goods, services, ideas, places, or persons.

THE MARKETING CONCEPT

The **Marketing Concept** is a customer-oriented business philosophy that stresses customer satisfaction as the key to achieving organizational goals. This philosophy maintains that all of the organization's efforts should be focused on identifying and satisfying the wants and needs of the customer.

MARKETING FUNCTIONS AND PROCESSES

There are six primary **Marketing Functions:**

1. Environmental Analysis
2. Consumer Analysis
3. Product Planning
4. Price Planning
5. Promotion Planning
6. Physical Distribution (Place) Planning

Environmental analysis and consumer analysis are market research functions that provide the means to evaluate market potential and identify target markets. Product, Price, Promotion, and Physical Distribution planning are known as the marketing mix variables.

The **Marketing Mix** is the combination of four variables that comprise an organization's marketing program: product, price, promotion, and physical distribution. The manner in which these factors are combined reflects the planned strategy of the organization. Unlike environmental forces, these factors are under the control of the organization. These are often referred to as the "four Ps."

Market Segmentation is the process of dividing the total market into distinct submarkets or groups based on similarities in their wants, needs, behaviors, or other characteristics.

Market Segments are groups of customers who are similar to each other in a meaningful way and who will respond to a firm's marketing mix similarly.

A **Target Market** is one particular group of potential customers that the organization seeks to satisfy with a product. It is the market at which the firm directs a marketing mix. Different marketing mixes are developed for each target market to satisfy their specific wants and needs. Target markets may be comprised of market segments or a mass market characterized by a "typical customer."

Product Differentiation exists when a product or brand is perceived as different from its competitors on any tangible or intangible characteristic. The term also refers to the strategy in which one firm promotes the features of its product over the features of competitive products in the same market.

Product Positioning refers to the decisions involved in shaping the product's image in the customer's mind. These images are defined relative to competing products. *Consumer perceptions* (not actual differences between products) are the critical issue. All elements of the marketing mix should be coordinated to achieve and support the firm's desired positioning of its brands. The effectiveness of changes in the marketing mix for a brand are evaluated by their contribution toward achieving the desired market position. Effective positioning relative to the needs and wants of a specific target market is the basis for competing effectively in most markets.

The **Marketing Plan** is the organization's statement of marketing strategy and the specification of the activities required to carry out the strategy. Marketing plans identify target markets and provide general guidelines for developing the marketing mix. Additional information in the plan may include environmental analysis, market research plans, cost estimates, and sales forecasts.

The process of developing a marketing plan begins with an assessment of the situation confronting the firm. This **situation analysis** identifies the company's relative strengths and weaknesses, as well as the opportunities and threats posed by its **marketing environment**. Based on this information, marketing objectives for specific products and markets are established. The development of the marketing mix reflects the objectives set for each product/market combination.

Marketing Objectives specify the goals of the firm in both quantitative (e.g., sales, profit, market share) and qualitative (e.g., market leadership, corporate image) terms. They reflect the role of marketing in achieving company-wide objectives. To be useful, marketing objectives must be specific, and measurable, and indicate the time period for which they are in effect. These goals are, in turn, translated into more detailed goals for marketing mix variables.

ENVIRONMENTAL ANALYSIS

The **Marketing Environment** is composed of two types of factors: those that the organization can control and those that it cannot control. The success of the firm in achieving its goals depends on the ability to understand the impact of uncontrollable factors, and the effective management of controllable factors in response.

External forces that impact all firms within an industry are termed **Macroenvironmental Factors**. These uncontrollable forces are

1. Demographics or Demography,
2. Economic Conditions,
3. Competition,
4. Social and Cultural Factors,
5. Political and Legal Factors (Government), and
6. Technological Factors.

Microenvironmental Factors are external forces that impact each specific company uniquely. Although these forces are largely uncontrollable, the firm can influence these factors to a significant degree. The microenvironmental factors are

1. Suppliers,
2. Marketing Intermediaries, and
3. The Target Market.

The factors over which the firm has direct control are internal resources and decision variables. Changes in the composition of the marketing mix and choice of target markets are the primary means by which the firm can respond to the uncontrollable factors in its environment.

MARKETING STRATEGY AND PLANNING

A firm's **Marketing Strategy** defines the way in which the marketing mix is used to satisfy the needs of the target market and achieve organizational goals. The Product/Market Opportunity Matrix, SWOT Matrix, and Boston Consulting Group Matrix provide guidelines to assess the relative value of products and product opportunities.

The **Product/Market Opportunity Matrix** specifies the four fundamental alternative marketing strategies available to the firm. The four types of opportunities identified by the matrix are a function of product and market factors.

	Present Markets	New Markets
Present Products	Market Penetration	Market Development
New Products	Product Development	Diversification

1. **Market Penetration Strategy** attempts to increase sales of the firm's existing products to its current markets.
2. **Market Development Strategy** attempts to increase sales by introducing existing products to new markets.
3. **Product Development Strategy** entails offering new products to the firm's current markets.
4. **Diversification Strategy** aims new products at new markets.

The **SWOT Matrix** is a tool used to assess the potential value and fit of new opportunities. Opportunities identified through the use of the Product/Market Opportunity Matrix should be judged against the strengths and weaknesses of the company relative to the threats and opportunities posed by the environment.

		INTERNAL	
		Strengths	Weaknesses
EXTERNAL	Opportunities		
	Threats		

Strengths – competitive advantages or distinctive competencies that give the firm a superior ability to meet the needs of its target markets

Weaknesses – limitations that a company might face in the development or implementation of a specific marketing strategy

Opportunities – favorable environmental conditions that could bring the firm rewards if exploited

Threats – competitive conditions or other barriers that might prevent the firm from reaching its goals

By plotting each of the opportunities under consideration in the matrix above, firms can identify those where internal company strengths match up well with external market opportunities—situations in the environment that represent the highest likelihood of success for the firm.

The **Boston Consulting Group Matrix** is a framework that classifies each product or product line within a firm's "product portfolio." The matrix identifies product categories as a function of their market shares relative to immediate competitors and growth rates for the industry.

		RELATIVE MARKET SHARE	
		High	Low
INDUSTRY GROWTH RATE	High	Star	Problem Child
	Low	Cash Cow	Dog

1. **Stars** generate large profits, but also consume substantial resources to finance their continued growth.

2. A **Problem Child** (sometimes called a "question mark") does not provide great profits, but still requires high levels of investment to maintain or increase market share.

3. **Cash Cows** generate large profits and require relatively little investment to maintain their market share in slow-growth industries.

4. **Dogs** are characterized by low profitability and little opportunity for sales growth.

A **Differential Advantage** is made up of the unique qualities of a product that encourage customer purchase and loyalty. It provides customers with substantive reasons to *prefer* one product over another. By contrast, product differentiation simply refers to consumers' ability to perceive differences among competing products.

Marketing Myopia is a term that is used to characterize short-sighted marketing strategy. It refers to the tendency of some marketing managers to focus narrowly on the products they sell rather than the customers they serve. Consequently, they lose sight of customer preferences as these wants and needs change over time.

A **Sustainable Competitive Advantage** is an enduring differential advantage held over competitors by offering buyers superior value either through lower prices or other elements of the marketing mix. Place or "location" is often regarded as the most sustainable competitive advantage since it is impossible for competitors to copy it.

2: MARKETING RESEARCH

Marketing Research is the systematic process of planning, collecting, analyzing, and communicating information that is relevant to making better marketing decisions.

Marketing Research is important to four primary activities: situation analysis, strategy development, marketing plan development, and monitoring the performance of plans following implementation.

Situation Analysis examines:

- Economic environment
- Technological developments
- Social changes, changes in buying behavior
- Legal and political developments
- Size of the existing market and the potential market
- Rate of market growth
- Buyer behavior
- Brand loyalty
- Competitive behavior
- Market share trends

Strategy Development questions addressed by marketing research include:

- What business should we be in?
- How will we compete?
- What are the goals for the business?

Marketing Plan Development issues focus on how the elements of the marketing mix can be most effectively used. In addition to investigations about the four p's, research of this type may also address questions about market segmentation, product differentiation, product positioning, and target market selection.

Monitoring the Performance of plans following implementation may require the collection of either qualitative or quantitative information. Measures of effectiveness may include sales, customer satisfaction, brand switching, and many others. The appropriate measure is dependent on the research question that managers are trying to answer.

The **Marketing Research Process** is designed to yield reliable and objective answers to specific marketing questions. The process can be described in six distinct steps.

Step 1: Define the Research Objective

What is the question to be answered and what information do you need?

Step 2: Determine Research Type

Exploratory: Identify problems or hypotheses

Descriptive: Information about existing market conditions

Causal: Identify cause-and-effect relationships

Step 3: Determine Research Approach

Qualitative: Observation, in-depth interviews, focus groups

Quantitative: Experiments, questionnaires

Step 4: Select Data Collection Method

Mail, telephone, personal interviews

Step 5: Analyze the Results

Step 6: Report the Findings

The **research design** specifies the plan for collecting and analyzing data. It explicitly identifies the nature of the data to be collected, the data-gathering procedures to be used, and the population to be studied.

Sampling is the process of gathering data from a selected subgroup (sample) chosen from the population of interest. If chosen properly, a sample of the population will accurately reflect the characteristics of the designated population. **Probability samples** select persons from the designated population at random. **Non-probability samples** are nonrandom samples.

Sample Size. Larger sample sizes yield more reliable results, but are also more expensive than smaller samples.

Primary v. Secondary Data. Primary data are information collected specifically for the current research study. Gathering primary data requires obtaining "new" information. **Secondary Data** consists of information that has already been collected for reasons not directly related to the current study. "Internal" secondary data is comprised of information available within the company. "External" secondary data is made up primarily of published sources.

Characteristics of Primary v. Secondary Data

	Primary Data	Secondary Data
Precisely Fits Firm's Needs	Yes	Seldom
Cost of Acquiring	Expensive	Low Cost
Speed in Collecting	Slow	Quick
Most Recent Information Possible	Yes	No
Multiple Sources	No	Often
Secrecy from Competitors	Yes	No

Survey Research is a means of systematically acquiring information from individuals by communicating directly with them. Surveys can be administered in person, by mail, or over the phone. **Focus Group** research is an in-person data collection procedure in which the interviewer meets with five to ten persons at the same time.

Characteristics of In-Person, Mail, and Phone Surveys

	In-Person	Mail	Phone
Response Rates	High	Low	High
Cost	Highest	Low	High
Potential Interviewer Bias	Yes	None	Yes
Follow-up Questions / Interactive	Yes	Yes	Yes
Respondents Willing to Spend Time	Yes	No	No
Speed of Data Collection	Fast	Slow	Fastest
Anonymity of Respondent	Lowest	High	Low

Observation is an unobtrusive data collection procedure. Subjects' behaviors are observed without their knowledge. Consequently, their cooperation is not required and their behaviors won't be influenced by the researcher. Its primary disadvantage is that individuals' attitudes cannot be known from observing behavior exclusively. Videotape recordings and checkout scanners in retail stores are two means of gathering observational data.

Experimental Research compares the impact of marketing variables on individuals' responses in a controlled setting. The primary advantage of experiments is that they can identify cause-and-effect relationships. The primary disadvantages are high costs and the artificiality of "laboratory" settings.

Simulation is a technique that utilizes computer-based programs to assess the impact of alternative marketing strategies. Mathematical models simulate real-world effects stemming from both the controllable and uncontrollable factors in the environment. The primary advantage to using simulations is that direct contact with the consumer is unnecessary. The validity of the assumptions made in constructing and using the models will determine the reliability and accuracy of the results obtained.

A **Marketing Information System** (MIS) is made up of the people, equipment, and procedures to gather, sort, analyze, evaluate, and distribute accurate information to marketing decision makers.

ESTIMATING MARKET DEMAND

A highly specialized function of Marketing Information Systems is **Forecasting**—estimating the demand for a brand or product category. Forecasts are predictions of what will happen in the future based on either qualitative or quantitative techniques. The qualitative techniques used in forecasting include:

- Internal expert opinion—often based on salespersons' knowledge of buyers
- Consulting panels of independent experts from outside the company
- Decision Trees and Scenario Building (probability models based on opinion)

Quantitative forecasting methods include:

- Sales forecasts based on the analysis and extension of historical trend data
- Mathematical models that incorporate multiple decision variables
- Multiple regression analysis
- Econometric modeling

Short-term forecasts typically predict sales for the next month or quarter and are used for production scheduling and evaluating the impact of short-term promotions. **Medium-term forecasts** are typically done annually and provide input to annual marketing plan review and revision. **Long-term forecasts** are typically done for a five-year period and play a significant role in strategic planning.

3: TARGET MARKETS

MARKET CHARACTERISTICS

To achieve the greatest benefit and competitive advantage from target marketing, it is essential that the characteristics used to identify each market be **measurable**. The characteristics used to specify target markets can be demographic or behavioral in nature.

DEMOGRAPHICS

Personal Demographics are the identifiable characteristics of individuals and groups of people. Personal demographic variables include age, sex, family size, income, occupation, and education. **Geographic Demographics** are the identifiable characteristics of towns, cities, states, regions, and countries. Geographic demographics include county size, city or SMSA (Standard Metropolitan Statistical Area) size, population density, and climate.

BEHAVIORAL DIMENSIONS

The behavior of individual consumers within target markets can be influenced by social factors, psychological variables, and purchase situations. These sources of influence can be used to describe and identify target markets. **Behavioral dimensions** of markets include purchase occasion, user status, user rate, and brand loyalty. Customer attitudes toward products and product benefits are also behavioral characteristics of markets.

Psychographics refer to those factors that influence consumers' patterns of living or lifestyle. These include activities, interests, opinions (AIOs), as well as social class, personality, and values.

MARKET SEGMENTATION

In most instances, the total potential market for a product is too diverse or **heterogeneous** to be treated as a single target market. **Market Segmentation** is the process by which the total potential market for a product is divided into smaller parts or segments. Segments are created by grouping customers together according to their characteristics or needs. The resulting segments are said to be **homogeneous** with respect to these dimensions. That is, potential buyers within each segment are more similar to each other on key dimensions than to buyers assigned to other segments. The objective is to identify groups that will respond in a similar manner to marketing programs.

The primary advantage to segmenting markets is that it allows marketers to better match products to the needs of different customer types. Developing a marketing mix tailored to a clearly defined target market will provide a competitive advantage for the firm. This advantage is gained by fitting the design of the product, promotional efforts, pricing, and distribution to the preferences of the customer.

The process of **segmenting** markets is performed in two steps. In the first stage, segmentation variables are chosen and the market is divided along these dimensions. This identifies groups of consumers who may require separate marketing mixes. The second stage requires profiling the resulting segments. Each segment is profiled according to its distinctive demographic and behavioral characteristics.

Once the segmentation process is complete, each resulting segment is evaluated in terms of its attractiveness for the firm. The firm's target market(s) are chosen based on this evaluation. This phase is referred to as **Market Targeting**.

In order to identify market segments that will respond in a homogeneous manner to marketing programs, three conditions must be satisfied:

1. The dimensions or bases used to segment the market must be **measurable**.

2. The market segment must be **accessible** or **reachable** through existing channels. These channels include advertising media, channels of distribution, and the firm's sales force.

3. Each segment must be **large enough** to be profitable. Whether or not a segment is potentially profitable will be affected by many factors including the nature of the industry, the size of the firm, and its pricing structure.

The most appropriate **variables** or **bases** for segmenting a market will vary from one product to another. The appropriateness of each potential factor in segmenting a market depends entirely on its relevance to the situation. The best segmentation bases are those that will identify meaningful differences between groups of customers.

Buyer behavior can seldom be adequately related to only one segmentation variable **(Single-Variable Segmentation)**. It is usually more appropriate to use two or more variables or "bases." **Multi-Variable Segmentation** recognizes the importance of interrelationships between factors in defining market segments. Common interrelationships can be observed between demographic factors such as age, income, and education.

Several factors will affect the firm's selection of **target markets**. Many of the factors that can be used in evaluating the potential and appropriateness of alternative segments are listed below.

Segment Characteristics	Competitors Within Segment	Match With Company
Size	Number	Strengths
Growth Potential	Size	Objectives
Profit Potential	Strength	Resources
	Resources	Channels

Managers may select one or more segments as their target markets. The decision to focus on one segment as a target market is called a **single-segment** or **concentration strategy**. The choice to pursue more than one target market with corresponding marketing mixes for each is called **multiple segmentation strategy**. This option is also sometimes called **differentiated marketing**. A third alternative is to treat the total potential market as a whole—one vast target market. This is referred to as **undifferentiated** or **mass marketing**.

CONSUMER BEHAVIOR

An understanding of consumer behavior is essential to the development of effective marketing programs. The creation of an appropriate marketing mix for a specific target market requires an understanding of consumer preferences and decision-making processes. Marketers also need to be aware of how they can influence consumers' decision-making through their use of marketing mix variables.

Consumers engage in many buying-related **behaviors**. Apart from purchasing products, consumers may spend significant time and effort in seeking out product information or shopping to compare alternative brands, stores, and prices. The primary determinant of how consumers reach purchase decisions is

involvement. Involvement refers to the importance that consumers attach to the purchase of a particular product.

There are several factors that may influence a consumer's level of involvement in a purchase situation. The characteristics most often associated with **high involvement** decision-making behavior are presented below.

- The product is perceived to be personally important.
- The product is relatively expensive or high-priced.
- The consumer lacks relevant information about the product.
- The risks associated with making a bad decision are high.
- The product offers potentially great benefits to the buyer.

On balance, most buying decisions tend to be **low involvement**. This is characteristic of frequently purchased, low-priced goods.

High Involvement Decision-Making can be characterized as a five-stage process. This process is shown below.

```
┌─────────────────────────────────────────────┐
│        Need or Problem Recognition          │
│                    ↓                         │
│        Search for Relevant Information       │
│                    ↓                         │
│   Identification and Evaluation of Alternatives │
│                    ↓                         │
│            Purchase Decision                 │
│                    ↓                         │
│          Postpurchase Behavior               │
└─────────────────────────────────────────────┘
```

One possible outcome of the purchase decision is postpurchase **cognitive dissonance**. This state of mental anxiety can be caused by a consumer's uncertainty about a purchase. Virtually all high-involvement decision processes generate a set of viable alternatives. Cognitive dissonance occurs when consumers continue to evaluate the advantages and disadvantages of alternatives after the sale has been made. Consequently, the buyer remains uncertain and less than fully satisfied with the final selection.

Low Involvement Decision-Making can be characterized as a three-stage process. This process is shown below.

```
Need or Problem Recognition
           ↓
     Purchase Decision
           ↓
  Postpurchase Behavior
```

Since the consequences of low-involvement decisions are less important to consumers, the processes of searching for relevant information and evaluating alternatives are generally omitted.

The distinction between high- and low-involvement decision-making is not intended to be absolute. High and low involvement represent the endpoints of a continuum. Many purchase decisions may share characteristics of both extremes. It is also worth noting that consumers are not all alike in this regard. What one may regard as an unimportant purchase may be very important to another.

Individuals' decision-making behavior is substantially influenced by many other factors within their environment. Consumer wants and perceptions are affected by social, psychological, and informational forces. Social factors include culture, social class, reference groups, and family members. Psychological factors involve consumer's motivations and personality. Informational forces provide decision makers with relevant views on products and brands in the marketplace. This information may stem from commercial sources (e.g., advertisers), independent sources (e.g., product rating services), or the consumer's social environment.

ORGANIZATIONAL AND INDUSTRIAL MARKETS

Organizational and industrial markets differ from consumer markets in the types of purchases made and the characteristics of the markets involved. Organizational buyers purchase materials for resale, operational needs, or for use in further production. Consumers most typically purchase finished goods for final consumption. Organizational consumers are fewer in number and are less geographically dispersed than final consumers.

One of the essential differences that separates organizational and consumer markets is **derived demand**. Organizational buyers derive their demand for materials from the anticipated demand by consumers for finished goods.

Some of the bases used to segment consumer markets also have applications in industrial and organizational markets (e.g., geographic demographics). There are three characteristics that are, however, used exclusively in segmenting non-consumer markets: **Customer Type**, **Customer Size**, and **Buying Situation**. Customer Types include manufacturers, wholesalers, retailers, government agencies, and nonprofit institutions. Customer Size is based on the purchasing power of buyers rather than the number of buyers. The Buying Situation can be characterized as one of three types: New-Task Buying, Straight Rebuy, or Modified Rebuy.

New-task buying is the most complex of the three buy classes. The task requires greater effort in gathering information and evaluating alternatives. More people are involved in the decision-making process for new-task buying than for the other two classes. New-task buying processes are most frequently employed in the purchase of high-cost products that the firm has not had previous experience with.

The **Straight Rebuy** process is used to purchase inexpensive, low-risk products. In most instances, previous purchases are simply reordered to replace depleted inventory. Alternative products or suppliers are not typically considered or evaluated.

Modified Rebuy processes are used when the purchase situation is less complex than new-task buying and more involved than a straight rebuy. Some information is required to reach decisions and a limited number of alternatives may be evaluated.

The sequence of stages in organizational decision making is similar to consumer purchasing. The high-involvement decision-making process for consumers is comparable to new-task buying within organizations. The five stages are the same. The fundamental difference is that more people are typically involved in reaching organizational buying decisions. Similarly, the three-stage model of low-involvement decision-making is comparable to organizational consumers' straight rebuy.

Organizational buying decisions are typically influenced by many people within the firm. Individuals who affect the decision-making process usually fit one of the categories listed below.

Buyers: Individuals who identify suppliers, arrange terms of sale, and carry out the purchasing procedures

Users: People within the firm who will use the product

Influencers: Those individuals who establish product requirements and specifications based on their technical expertise or authority within the organization

Gatekeepers: People within the organization who control the flow of relevant purchase-related information

Deciders: The individual(s) who makes the final purchase decision

The **Buying Center** is not a specific place or location within an organization. It is an entity comprised of all the people who participate in or influence the decision-making process. The number of people making up the buying center will vary between organizations. Within an organization, it will change with the nature and complexity of the purchase under consideration. Large companies may establish a formal "buying committee" to evaluate purchasing policies and product line modifications.

4: PRODUCT PLANNING AND MANAGEMENT

Product Planning entails all phases of decision making related to new product development and the management of existing products. The role of product-related factors in marketing is to provide goods and services that will satisfy the demands of the market and create a profit for the firm. The dynamics of product management are shaped by changing tastes and preferences within the market.

PRODUCT CLASSIFICATION

Products can be classified as either **consumer products** or **industrial products** depending on their markets. Consumer products are targeted toward individuals and households for final consumption. Industrial products, sometimes called **business products**, are typically purchased for resale, operational needs, or use in further production.

Consumer goods can be further classified into one of three product types: Convenience, Shopping, and Specialty. **Convenience goods** are those purchased frequently and with a minimum of shopping effort (low-involvement decision-making). **Shopping goods** are those for which consumers typically make price-quality comparisons at several stores before buying (high-involvement decision-making). **Specialty goods** are those for which buyers have strong brand loyalty—they'll accept no substitutes. Shopping behavior for these products is characterized by doing "whatever it takes" to find and purchase their brand. The characteristics corresponding to each type of product are illustrated below.

Product Characteristics	Type of Product		
	Convenience	Shopping	Specialty
Effort Expended in Shopping for Product	Very Little	Moderate	As Much As Needed
Information Search and Evaluation of Alternatives	Very Little	High	Very Little
Product Importance or Involvement	Low	High	Varies
Price	Usually Low	Usually High	Varies
Frequency of Purchase	High	Low	Varies
Willingness to Accept Substitutes	High	Moderate	None

An additional category used for a very unusual class of consumer products is **unsought goods**. Unsought goods are those for which no demand exists. This may be due to the fact these are new and unfamiliar product innovations or simply because consumers do not currently want them.

Industrial or **Business Goods** can be classified as belonging to one of six product categories. The categories are based on the uses of the products and purchase characteristics. **Raw Materials**, **Component Materials**, and **Fabricated Parts** are used in the production of finished goods or become part of them. **Accessory Equipment** and **Installations** are capital goods that are used in the production process (e.g., assembly line equipment, drill presses, lathes). **Operating Supplies** are low-cost items that aid in the production process (e.g., lubricating oils, pencils, janitorial supplies). The characteristics corresponding to each type of product are illustrated in the table below.

Product Type	Unit Price	Frequency of Purchase	Becomes a Part of Final Product	Complexity of the Decision-Making Process
Raw Materials	Very Low	High	Often	Low
Component Materials	Low	Varies	Yes	Low
Fabricated Parts	Low	Varies	Yes	Low
Accessory Equipment	Medium	Low	No	Medium
Installations	Very High	Very Low	No	Very High
Operating Supplies	Low	High	No	Low

Services are tasks performed by one individual or firm for another. Services may be classified as either **consumer services** or **industrial services**, depending on the customers served. Services may be provided in conjunction with goods (e.g., auto rental) or without (e.g., accounting services). There are three tendencies that are characteristic of services. Services are **often intangible**. Services are **usually perishable**. Unlike products, they cannot be stored for use at a later date. Services are **frequently inseparable** from the individual(s) who provide the service (e.g., accounting services). Many services (e.g., medical) also require that the customer receive the services at the site where they are provided.

PRODUCT CONCEPTS

Products are defined within marketing as bundles of attributes. These attributes include both tangible and intangible product features. Products may be goods or services. They are the consequence of the firm's efforts to satisfy both consumer and organization goals.

The **Tangible Product** consists of those features that can be precisely specified (e.g., color, size, weight). The **Extended** or **Augmented Product** includes both the tangible and intangible elements of a product. These intangible features would include brand image and accompanying service features.

A firm's **Product Line** consists of a group or set of closely related items. Product lines usually share some attributes in common. Some of the features that may relate items within a line include product composition, customers, and distribution channels. A firm's **Product Mix** is comprised of all the product lines that it offers.

NEW PRODUCT PLANNING

New Product Opportunities can stem from the modification of existing products or the development of wholly new product innovations. New products can make important contributions to the growth, profitability, and competitiveness of the firm. The illustration below shows the range of possible new product opportunities.

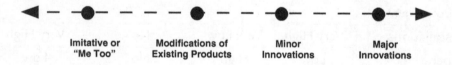

| Imitative or "Me Too" | Modifications of Existing Products | Minor Innovations | Major Innovations |

Imitative, "Me Too," or "Cloned" products are not typically regarded as innovative. They are not new to the market. They are only new to the firm attempting to enter a new market with a copy of competitors' products.

Idea Generation is the process of searching for new product opportunities. There are many methods used to generate new ideas including laboratory studies, market research, and "**brainstorming**." Brainstorming is a small-group technique that encourages participants to voice creative ideas on a specified topic. The idea generation process may involve experts within the firm as well as consumers and experts from outside the company. Employees at all levels, suppliers, distributors, and others knowledgeable about the products and markets involved may participate in the process.

Product Screening and Concept Testing takes place after the firm has generated several ideas for new products. In the **Product Screening** phase, potential products are sorted relative to their strengths and weaknesses. After those failing to meet the firm's standards are eliminated from further consideration, the remaining concepts are tested. **Concept Testing** subjects new ideas to consumer scrutiny. Potential customers for the new product are asked to evaluate the concept. Their attitudes toward the idea partially determine whether or not there is sufficient consumer interest and sales potential to warrant further development of the product.

Business Analysis and Product Development are the next two stages in the process for those product concepts that survive the screening and concept testing phases. **Business Analysis** is a detailed evaluation of the concept's commercial feasibility. The criteria examined at this stage include product costs, competitors' strengths in relevant markets, projected market demand, needed investment, and potential profitability. **Product Development** is the stage at which viable ideas are first produced in tangible form and the initial marketing strategy is created. Initial product models may continue to undergo testing and refinement at this stage as well.

Test Marketing and Commercialization are the final stages in the process of developing new products. **Test Marketing** provides a series of commercial experiments to test the acceptance of the product and the appropriateness of the proposed marketing strategy. These limited studies are conducted in one or more isolated geographic markets. Information from test markets is used to further refine the marketing strategy and, if needed, the product itself. If product sales have been adequate in test markets, the next stage is **Commercialization**. Commercialization marks the start of full-scale production and the implementation of the complete marketing plan. This step corresponds to the Introduction stage of the Product Life Cycle for the product.

PRODUCT ADOPTION AND DIFFUSION

After a product has been introduced, the firm's initial objective is to gain consumer acceptance. The **Product Adoption Process** describes the stages that consumers go through in learning about new products. The process begins with a prospect's initial awareness of the product. If interested, the prospect will evaluate the perceived merits of the product and develop an opinion or attitude toward trying the product. If this attitude is sufficiently positive, the individual may buy the product (initial product trial). This trial will either confirm or reverse the buyer's initially positive impression. **Product Adoption** takes place when the buyer decides to continue using the product regularly. Despite having adopted the product, buyers seek regular reassurance or confirmation that their decision to adopt the product was a correct one.

The **Diffusion Process** describes the typical rate of adoption exhibited by consumers in response to new products. There are five categories of adopters.

- **Innovators** are the first to buy a new product. They comprise approximately three percent of the relevant market. They tend to be younger, more affluent, and more cosmopolitan than later clusters of buyers.

- **Early Adopters** are the next to buy. They make up approximately 13 percent of consumers. Early Adopters tend to be more locally oriented than innovators and are typically well respected within their communities. They are opinion leaders who influence others' buying patterns.

- The **Early Majority** represent about 34 percent of the target market. They tend to be slightly above average in both social and economic standing. They are influenced by advertising and salespeople, as well as Early Adopters.

- The **Late Majority** represent another 34 percent of the market. They are more resistant to change and risk taking than previous groups. They tend to be middle aged or older and somewhat less well off than average in socioeconomic terms.

- **Laggards** make up 16 percent of the market and are the last to buy. They tend to be price conscious, low-income consumers. By the time Laggards have adopted the product, it has reached the Maturity stage of the Product Life Cycle.

PRODUCT MIX MANAGEMENT

Product Positioning refers to the process of developing a product or brand image in the consumer's mind. The image is defined as a **position** relative to competing brands and products. Positioning is based on consumer perceptions of product features relative to their preferences. **Ideal points** identify consumers' perception of the perfect bundle or combination of attributes.

Firms may expand their product mix by adding new lines or increasing the depth of existing product lines. **Mix expansion** provides the firm with new opportunities for growth. Firms may also consider reducing or **contracting** the product mix. This can be accomplished either by eliminating entire lines or reducing the variety within lines. This weeding out process is usually intended to eliminate products that provide low profits.

The relationship between product lines within the same firm can be used to secure competitive advantages in the marketplace. A **wide product mix** represents a diversification strategy. Offering several different product lines enables the firm to meet several different types of customer needs. **Deep product mixes** focus the firm's resources on a smaller number of product lines. In turn, this allows the development of several products within each line. The firm can then target several segments within the same market.

PRODUCT LIFE CYCLE

The Product Life Cycle describes a pattern of changes that is characteristic of most products from their inception to their eventual departure from the market. The life cycle is divided into four stages: Introduction, Growth, Maturity, and Decline. The product's movement through each stage is described in terms of its sales, profits, and competitors.

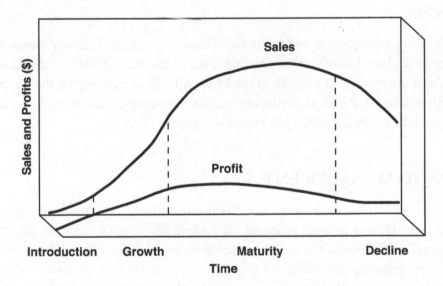

Introduction

This stage of the Product Life Cycle (PLC) corresponds to the commercialization of a new product. The rate of new product failures during this stage remains high. Sales, beginning at $0, increase steadily throughout the Introduction stage, though profits remain negative. Innovators are the initial buyers of the product. There is very little direct competition in this phase.

Growth

The beginning of the Growth stage is marked by the point at which profitability becomes positive. Sales growth continues at an increasing rate and new firms will enter the market, attracted by high-profit potential.

Maturity

The initial phase of the Maturity stage is characterized by slowing sales. Eventually industry sales level off as the market becomes saturated. Consumer demand peaks during this stage. Price competition is greater during maturity than during the preceding stages. Some manufacturers may be forced out of the market as total industry profits decrease throughout maturity.

Decline

Industry sales decline and many firms leave the market. Industry profits continue to decline throughout the Decline stage of the PLC. Most remaining firms will exit the market. The length of the PLC will vary depending on the nature of the product, technological displacement, the competitive climate, and consumer demand. In general, product life cycles are getting shorter.

BRAND MANAGEMENT

A brand is a name or symbol that is used to identify the products of a specific firm. Brands provide products with identification. The identity and "personality" of the product is created around the brand name. Strong brand names can also enhance the image of the parent company and enhance consumer acceptance of new products introduced under the same name.

Brands make shopping simpler for consumers. They ensure that shoppers can repeat purchases of products that they prefer (brand loyalty). The brand name provides implicit assurance that the quality will remain unchanged over time. Brand images also serve to differentiate competitors. Consequently, price comparisons become less critical in consumers' decision making and other differences enter into the evaluation process. Consumers also tend to feel more confident and secure when buying a familiar brand. Distinctive brands can provide the centerpiece around which marketing strategies are developed.

Different types of brands are classified according to their origin. **Manufacturer brands** are created by product manufacturers. These are sometimes called "National Brands." **Dealer Brands** are created by intermediaries (e.g., retailers). These are sometimes referred to as "Private Brands."

Characteristics of Good Brand Names:

- Suggests something about the product's benefits
- Short and simple
- Easy to spell, read, and pronounce
- Pleasant sounding
- Distinctive and memorable
- Appropriate to new products that may be added to the line at a later date
- Legally available for use

Brand Familiarity exists on five different levels:

- Brand Insistence occurs when consumers are absolutely brand loyal and will accept no substitutes.
- Brand Preference means that target consumers will usually choose one specific brand over others.
- Brand Recognition exists when consumers remember the brand name.
- Brand Non-Recognition means that consumers do not recall the brand name.
- Brand Rejection exists when consumers recognize, but refuse to buy, specific brands.

Marketers of more than one product have several branding strategies to consider. A **Family Brand** strategy is used when the same brand is applied to several products. Family branding is most appropriate when all of the products are of comparable type and quality. **Individual Brands** can be assigned to each product when there exists significant variation in product type and quality. Generic products are those that have no brand name at all. Intermediaries often market low-priced generic products to cost-conscious consumers.

A Licensed Brand is a well-established brand name that other sellers pay to use. This allows sellers to take advantage of existing brand recognition and preferences.

Trademarks are brand names, marks, or characters used to identify products. Registered trademarks are legally protected entities—reserved for the exclusive use of their owners.

PACKAGING

Packaging serves valuable functions for both buyers and sellers. The three primary functions of product packaging are **Protection**, **Promotion**, and **Information**.

Effective packaging can prevent product damage and spoiling. The costs associated with good packaging are partially offset by the resulting reduction in goods damaged in transit. Child-proof and tamper-resistant protective packaging can also provide additional benefits to the final consumer.

Packaging can be an effective promotional tool. Consumers are exposed to product packaging at the point-of-purchase. Consequently, it represents the last opportunity to influence their decision making. Distinctive packages that reinforce positive brand images help sell the product.

Benefits provided by the packaging itself can also enhance consumer preference. Improved dispensers, reusable containers, and greater convenience are examples of how packaging can increase the value of the purchase.

Product Information and Labeling permit consumers to critically evaluate products and compare brands. Consumers are increasingly concerned with product contents, nutritional information, and the environmental consequences of the products and packaging they purchase.

Services Marketing differs from the marketing of goods in several ways and poses unique challenges. Legal and medical services are typical examples. Services are distinct from manufactured goods in four ways: intangibility, inseparability, perishability, and variability.

Services are **intangible** because they are not experienced by buyers until the service is performed. This makes it difficult for clients to understand them or evaluate their quality. Service providers find it difficult to display or communicate relevant information about their services and often have trouble setting prices.

Inseparability refers to the fact that the service cannot be separated from the person providing it. The quality of service is unique and dependent on the skills of the service provider. This is because the client must participate in the production of the service.

Services are **perishable** because they cannot be inventoried, returned, or resold. Sales lost during off-peak times represent revenue that is lost forever.

Services are **variable** because they are not performed in the same way each and every time. This raises the level of perceived risk for buyers of services.

5: DISTRIBUTION SYSTEMS

CHANNELS OF DISTRIBUTION

Channels of distribution are designed in response to the needs of the sellers in executing the marketing mix. Environmental factors considered within this context include company resources, buyer behavior, competitors' strategies, and the product itself. Channel structure, the relative intensity of distribution, and the number of members within the channel are among the critical decisions made in establishing a distribution channel.

CHANNEL FUNCTIONS

The physical distribution of products is the primary function served by channels. Distribution includes transportation, inventory management, and customer service functions. Intermediaries can also perform other tasks that contribute to greater channel efficiency and market development. These include market research, promotion, and product planning.

In many channel systems, members participate in the **sorting** process. This includes accumulation, sorting, and assorting functions. **Accumulation** is the process of assembling and pooling relatively small individual shipments so that they can be transported more economically. **Sorting** is the process of separating goods by quality, color, or size. **Assorting** is typically performed at the retail level. It is the process of acquiring a wide variety of merchandise to meet the diverse preferences of consumers.

CHANNEL STRUCTURE

Channel systems that move goods from the producer to the final consumer without using independent intermediaries or "middlemen" are termed **Direct Channels**. Those that move goods with the cooperation and assistance of independent intermediaries are **Indirect Channels**.

Channel width refers to the number of independent members at one level of the distribution channel (e.g., producer, wholesaler, retailer, final consumer). **Channel length** refers to the number of levels used to create a distribution channel.

The intensity of a distribution system is determined by the number of intermediaries involved at the wholesale and retail levels of the channel. An **Intensive** distribution strategy is one in which a firm sells through every potential outlet that will reach its target market. With **Selective** distribution, a firm will sell through many, but not all, potential wholesalers and retailers. An **Exclusive** distribution strategy limits the number of outlets employed to one or two intermediaries within each market.

Three types of systems can be used to coordinate distribution functions within indirect channels. In a **Corporate** channel of distribution, one firm owns either all channel members or the firms at the next level in the channel. The control of operations within the channel is maintained through ownership.

Two arrangements can be used to coordinate the functions of independent members within indirect channels. **Contractual** arrangements specify performance terms for each independent channel member. Legal contracts specify terms governing the matters related to the physical movement of goods, pricing policies, and system efficiency. **Administered** arrangements coordinate channel operations through a dominant channel member. The market power of the dominant firm is sufficient to secure the voluntary cooperation of other channel members.

Vertical Integration is the process of acquiring firms that operate at different channel levels. One possible outcome of this strategy is the development of a corporate channel system. In this instance, vertical integration has the effect of increasing operational control and stability of the channel. **Horizontal Integration** is the process of acquiring firms that operate at the same channel level. This strategy allows the firm to increase its competitive strength, market share, and power within the channel system.

MULTIPLE CHANNELS

Multiple Channels (also called dual distribution) exist when a firm develops two or more separate and distinct distribution channels. This strategy may be pursued for several reasons. The firm may use multiple channels as a means of increasing market coverage or to reach new market segments. New channels may also be created to distribute new products.

CHANNEL BEHAVIOR

Channel Control refers to the ability to influence the actions of other channel members. This control may be established by the decision-making structure of the channel (e.g., corporate ownership) or from the relative market power of the members.

Channel Conflict exists when disagreements arise between members over channel practices and policies. Horizontal conflicts take place between firms at the same channel level. Vertical conflict occurs between firms at different levels of the same distribution system.

PUSHING vs. PULLING STRATEGIES

Manufacturers have two strategy alternatives to consider as a means of ensuring that products (especially new products) reach the final consumer. **Pushing** a product through the channel utilizes promotional efforts to secure the cooperation of intermediaries. Sales promotions, personal selling, and advertising are directed toward persuading intermediaries to cooperate in the marketing of the product. A **Pulling** strategy generates consumer demand for the product as a means of securing support within the channel. Promotional efforts are initially directed toward the final consumer. Pulling is most appropriate for new products seeking to gain access to an existing channel.

PHYSICAL DISTRIBUTION SYSTEMS

The most fundamental physical distribution tasks are transportation, materials handling, order processing, and inventory management. The goals of physical distribution systems are most critically concerned with two interrelated issues: costs and customer service. Cost control and reduction can be achieved through more efficient transportation practices and improved inventory management. Customer service and customer satisfaction depends on the efficient processing of orders and the reliable delivery of goods.

The **Total-Cost Concept** recognizes that minimizing costs and satisfying customer demands can represent conflicting objectives. The goal of the Total-Cost approach to system efficiency is to provide a level of customer service at the lowest total costs. These costs include lost sales resulting from customer dissatisfaction. The Total-Cost Concept takes into account that sacrificing some marginal sales opportunities can result in lower total system costs. Consequently, the ideal physical distribution system must strike a balance that preserves both high sales opportunities, customer satisfaction, and the lowest possible distribution costs.

Providing one centrally located stock of inventory for all markets provides for better inventory control, requires less total inventory, and reduces handling costs. This strategy may, however, create very high transportation costs and delivery delays for customers. Using too many dispersed inventory sites poses the opposite problems.

The **Distribution-Center Concept** recognizes that the most effective strategy may be a compromise between these two extremes. The resulting **distribution centers** are a type of warehouse planned in relation to specific markets. They provide key locations at which all operations take place. Each center is an integrated system that takes orders, processes them, and makes delivery to the customer.

Suboptimization refers to cost-reducing actions in one distribution function that increase the overall cost of other distribution functions.

Customer Service Standard refers to different customers requiring different levels of service. Service needs vary from buyer to buyer and sellers need to analyze and adapt to customer preferences. The basic dimensions that relate to customer service in distribution include fair prices, dependable product delivery, timeliness, availability, adequacy of inventory in stock, efficient order processing, replacement of defective goods, and warranties.

Order Processing refers to the receipt and transmission of sales order information. The primary tasks involved in order processing include order entry, order handling, and order delivery. **Electronic Data Interchange** (EDI) allows a company to integrate order processing, production, inventory planning, and transportation into a single system.

Materials Handling refers to the physical handling of goods in both warehouse and transportation functions. **Unit loading** refers to the grouping of boxes on a pallet or skid. **Containerization** is the process of consolidating many items into one container.

Warehousing is the process of designing and operating facilities for both storing and moving goods. Warehouse functions include receiving, sorting, storing, and dispatching goods. Types of **warehouses** include private and public warehouses, distribution centers, and bonded storage. Concepts related to the efficient operation of warehouses and warehouse inventory management include:

> **Order Leadtime** – the average length of time between the customer placing an order and receiving it
>
> **Reorder Point** – the inventory level at which new orders need to be placed to avoid a stockout
>
> **Stockout** – a shortage of product resulting from carrying too few in inventory
>
> **Usage Rate** – the rate at which inventory is sold per time period
>
> **Safety Stock** – the amount of extra inventory kept on hand to avoid stockouts
>
> **Economic Order Quantity (EOQ)** – the order size that minimizes the total cost of ordering and carrying inventory
>
> **Just-in-Time (JIT)** – making products and materials available just as needed for production or resale

Transportation Modes – the means of moving goods from one location to another. The five major modes are railroads, trucks, waterways, airways, and pipelines.

Megacarriers – freight transport companies that provide several shipment modes

Intermodal Transportation – two or more transportation modes used in combination

Freight Forwarders – specialized agencies that provide alternate forms of transportation coordination

6: WHOLESALING AND RETAILING

WHOLESALING

Wholesaling consists of all the activities related to the resale of products to organizational buyers, other wholesalers, and retailers. These functions typically include warehousing, transporting, and financing. Wholesalers participate in the sorting process by accumulating an assortment of merchandise and redistributing large product volumes in smaller units. Wholesalers provide a sales force that enables manufacturers to reach many customers at relatively low costs.

Manufacturer Wholesaling exists when the product's producer performs the wholesaling functions. These are carried out through the manufacturer's branch offices and sales offices. **Merchant Wholesalers** are independent firms that take title and possession of the products they sell. These firms are sometimes referred to as distributors or jobbers. Merchant wholesalers may be full- or limited-service wholesalers.

Full-Service Merchant Wholesalers perform the complete range of wholesaling functions. They store, promote, and transport merchandise. They provide sales support, merchandising assistance, customer service, and market research information to both their suppliers and customers. They can often provide assistance in financing transactions by extending trade credit. **Limited-Service Merchant Wholesalers** may not provide merchandising or market research assistance. In most instances, they will not extend credit to facilitate transactions.

Rack Jobbers are full-service merchant wholesalers that provide the display racks used to merchandise the product. **Drop Shippers** are limited-service merchant wholesalers that buy products from manufacturers and arrange for the delivery to retailers. They take title of the merchandise, but do not take physical possession of it.

Agents are independent wholesalers that do not take title of the products that they handle. They derive their compensation through sales commissions or manufacturer fees. **Brokers** act as temporary wholesalers. Their primary function is to bring buyers and sellers together and facilitate the transaction process. They do not take title of merchandise.

RETAILING

Retailing consists of all the activities related to the sale of products to final consumers for individual or household consumption. Retailers are the final link in the channel of distribution.

There are three forms of **Ownership** that can be used to classify retailers. **Corporate Chains** are comprised of several (usually 10 or more) stores that are owned and managed by the same firm. They are typically standardized with respect to product tines, merchandising, and operational policies.

Vertical Marketing Systems provide a collective means of enhancing the market power of individually owned retail units. Vertical Marketing Systems (VMS's) link stores together in voluntary chains or cooperatives. These contractual arrangements allow the group to compete more effectively and provide members with the advantages enjoyed by chain stores. The VMS provides members with assistance in merchandising, personnel training, inventory management, accounting, and promotion.

Independent Stores are single retail units that are not affiliated with a corporate chain or cooperative. They tend to have higher prices than affiliated stores, less market power, and rely more heavily on customer service for a competitive edge.

Franchise Systems are a specific type of Vertical Marketing System. Under this form of VMS, the parent company (franchisor) provides franchisees with the legal right to use company trademarks. The franchisor may also provide franchisees with assistance in site selection, personnel training, inventory management, and promotional strategy. This system allows franchisees to take advantage of well-known product and brand names. Participants may also benefit from the direct acquisition of proven store layouts and operational procedures.

Retail stores may pursue one of several store mix strategies. These strategies are based on product assortment, pricing strategy, and the level of customer service provided. The table below classifies each store according to the width and depth of its product assortment, pricing strategy, and level of customer service relative to other store types selling similar products.

Store Type	Product Assortment	Pricing Strategy	Customer Service
Convenience Store	Narrow/Shallow	High Prices	Low
Supermarket	Wide/Deep	Low/Moderate	Moderate
Department Store	Wide/Deep	Moderate	Moderate/High
Discount Store	Wide/Shallow	Low	Low
Specialty Store	Narrow/Very Deep	High	High
Catalog Showroom	Wide/Shallow	Low	Low
Superstores & Hypermarkets	Very Wide/Deep	Low	Low

Nonstore Retailing describes retail transactions that occur outside of traditional store settings. The techniques of nonstore retailing include direct selling, direct marketing, and vending sales. These activities account for about 20 percent of retail sales.

The selection of a **retail store location** is a function of the target market, location of competitors, and site costs. Location options include planned shopping centers, unplanned business/shopping districts, and isolated store locations.

A store's **atmosphere** is comprised of those characteristics that contribute to consumers' general impression of the store—its image. The dimensions that contribute to store atmosphere include the exterior appearance, interior design, product display, and store layout.

Scrambled Merchandising takes place as retailers add products that are not related to their traditional lines. Retailers engaged in this practice are seeking to add any products that sell quickly, increase profitability, and build store traffic. Scrambled merchandising can attract different target markets and often creates competition between unrelated retail stores.

Wheel of Retailing is a concept that describes the evolution of retail stores. The theory states that new retailers enter markets as low-status, low-price competitors. If successful, they tend to evolve into more traditional forms—adding customer-service features and raising prices to meet higher operating costs. This moving-up process creates opportunities for new retailers to enter the market with "low-end" strategies.

Non-store Retailing or **Direct Marketing** is two-way interaction between a marketer and individual consumers to both obtain an immediate response and cultivate lasting customer relationships. These channels include Internet marketing, catalog marketing, direct mail, infomercials, TV home shopping channels, and other forms of direct marketing. The growth in direct marketing sales over the past decade can be attributed to:

- Consumers' lack of time, combined with the convenience of ordering from direct marketers
- The higher costs of driving, traffic, and parking congestion
- Growth of customer databases in both number and sophistication
- Demassification—the focus on smaller market segments and niches

7: PROMOTIONAL STRATEGY

PROMOTION PLANNING

The process of Promotion Planning requires that the firm identify the most appropriate Promotion Mix, Objectives, and Budget. The Promotion Plan serves to coordinate elements of the firm's promotional efforts with the total marketing program. Elements within the promotional mix must be both internally consistent and jointly supportive of the strategic direction of the other marketing mix variables.

Promotion Mix is comprised of those elements that contribute to the firm's overall communications program. The mix includes advertising, personal selling, publicity, public relations, and sales promotions.

Integrated Marketing Communications (IMC) refers to the concept of planning a comprehensive program that coordinates all promotional activities. IMC programs specify four W's:

- Who is the target market?
- What are the objectives?
- When should the promotions be run?
- Which media should be used?

Promotion Objectives may address three goals within the marketing mix. Promotion can be used to **inform** both intermediaries and end-users about new products. For products that are already established, promotion can be used to persuade buyers. The objective is to influence brand preference and purchase behavior. Promotion may also serve to **remind** buyers about the availability of very well-established products.

Communication Channels provide the medium through which promotional messages are sent and delivered. The elements of a typical channel of communication are shown on the following page.

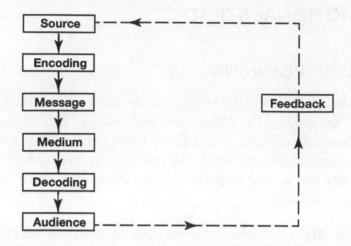

This process may be interfered with or could break down at any point along the sequence due to **noise**. Noise may result in poorly encoded/decoded messages or weak audience response.

Several different techniques can be used to establish promotion **budgets**. The **Percent-of-Sales** technique allocates a fixed percentage of the previous year's sales for promotional programs. The **Competitive Parity** approach establishes a budget based on the actions of the firm's closest competitors. This strategy seeks to mirror rivals' changes in promotional intensity. The **Objective and Task** procedure relies on the matching of promotional objectives to the funding required to achieve specific, objective-related tasks.

New firms often spend as much as they can afford when initially establishing a promotion budget. Once all other elements of the marketing plan have been funded, the **All Available Funds** technique allocates remaining resources to promotional activities.

ADVERTISING PLAN

Advertising **objectives** are determined by the marketing strategy for the product or firm. These objectives may include:

- New Product Introduction—Build Brand Awareness
- Establish Brand Preference (Selective Demand)
- Create and Maintain Brand Loyalty
- Market Development
- Build Primary Demand, Industry Sales

- Increase Product Uses or Rates of Usage
- Support the Firm's Sales Force
- Enhance the Firm's Image

Several of these objectives are typically combined in the development of an advertising plan.

The **Advertising Budget** stems from the budget developed in the Promotion Plan. The determination of a specific dollar allocation reflects the costs associated with alternative media and production costs.

Two different levels of decision making relate to **media planning**: the choice of media-type and the selection of specific vehicles within each medium. Once appropriate vehicles have been identified, the process of developing advertising schedules and buying media begins.

The alternative media available to advertisers include television, radio, newspapers, magazines, outdoor advertising, and direct mail. Each medium has distinctive characteristics that may pose an advantage or problem—depending on the creative requirements of the ad and the nature of the product.

Medium	Strengths	Weaknesses
Television	Combines action and sound. Extensive market coverage.	Very expensive. Viewers' short attn. span.
Radio	Station formats can provide access to target markets.	Audio only. Very passive medium.
Newspapers	Flexible—short lead times. Concentrated market.	Poor-quality printing. High ad clutter.
Magazines	High-quality color printing. Very selective means of access to specific audiences. Long life, good pass-along value.	Less flexible scheduling of ads—long lead times.
Outdoor Ads	High-intensity coverage within geographic market area. Large size, brief messages.	Low impact. Public criticism of "landscape pollution."
Direct Mail	Highly selective—no wasted circulation.	Low rate of consumer acceptance. Very expensive.

The selection of specific vehicles within each medium can be influenced by several factors. The evaluation of alternative vehicles is based on the cost and market coverage measures listed below.

Reach refers to the percentage of a target audience that is exposed to an ad through a given vehicle, within a specified time frame. The time frame used is typically four weeks.

Advertising costs are evaluated according to the cost of reaching a thousand prospects through a given vehicle—**Cost-per-Thousand**. Establishing this common measure of efficiency allows for comparisons across media and within media types.

Frequency refers to the average number of times that members of the target audience are exposed to an ad through a given vehicle. Like Reach, Frequency is usually based on a four-week period.

Gross Rating Points (GRPs) are calculated by multiplying Reach times Frequency. GRPs indicate the "total weight" of advertising delivered over a four-week period.

The **Creative Platform** provides the overall concept and theme for an advertising campaign. Themes may relate to the product, the consumer, or the firm. Product themes emphasize performance characteristics and the brand's competitive advantages. Consumer themes stress benefits of using the brand or illustrate how the product can enhance the buyer's life. Ads emphasizing the firm are typically intended to improve the image of the company.

Advertising Effectiveness can be assessed by both direct and indirect measures. Sales, store traffic, and coupon redemption rates provide direct measures of advertising effects. Indirect measures use consumers' recall of ads to estimate their impact.

PUBLICITY AND PUBLIC RELATIONS

Publicity is a form of nonpersonal communication that is not paid for by an identified sponsor. Publicity efforts initiated by firms include news features, articles in business and trade publications, and editorials. Publicity about a firm may be either positive or negative. The content of publicity pieces can be influenced, but not controlled, by a firm. Both positive and negative publicity is characterized by high audience attentiveness and high credibility.

Public Relations may be paid or nonpaid and includes both personal and nonpersonal communications. Public relations is primarily concerned with enhancing the image of the firm. Institutional advertising, personal appearances, and publicity represent various forms of public relations.

PERSONAL SELLING

There are three types of salespeople corresponding to the essential tasks of personal selling. **Order Getters** are responsible for securing new business for the firm. **Order Takers** service customer accounts that have already been established.

There are two types of **Support Salespeople** who provide assistance to both the order getters and order takers. Missionary salespeople work for producers. They foster goodwill and work to maintain productive relationships with intermediaries and their customers. Technical Specialists support the efforts of order getters and order takers by providing customers with expert technical assistance.

The process of recruiting salespeople begins with determining the number of people needed and the qualifications desired. These factors may include education, intelligence, technical knowledge/skills, job experience, and personality traits. Based on a written job description, a pool of qualified applicants is reviewed and the best qualified candidates should be selected.

Sales force training programs differ, according to the needs of the employer. Virtually all salespeople need some training. The most fundamental issues in training programs include company policies, product information, and selling techniques.

Sales potential, the maximum possible sales within a territory, will vary according to several considerations. Some of these factors include the number of potential buyers, the size of accounts, the relative dispersion of buyers, and the geographic characteristics of the market.

Sales Force Allocation to specific territories should attempt to match the talent and ability of salespeople to the characteristics of the customers within the territory. Ideally, each salesperson should be assigned to the territory where his or her relative contribution to the firm's profitability is the greatest. Sales managers will endeavor to minimize the ratio of selling expense to total sales for each territory.

Selling Process is a sequence of stages that are essential to effective personal selling.

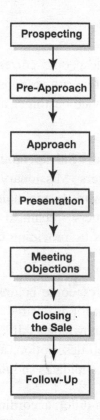

Prospecting is the process of seeking and identifying prospective buyers or "leads." In addition, the prospect must be "qualified" to buy. In **Qualifying Leads** the salesperson determines whether the prospect is both willing and able to buy.

The **Pre-Approach** takes place prior to meeting with a qualified prospect, when the salesperson must decide how to best initiate a face-to-face meeting. This includes an analysis of available information about the prospect's buying behavior and an evaluation of competitors' products.

The **Approach** takes place when the seller first meets the prospective buyer. The goal at this stage is to gain the interest and attention of the buyer. Since there are several possible strategies that can be effective, careful pre-approach planning should indicate which ones are most likely to succeed.

The **Presentation** of the sales message may take the form of a prepared ("canned") presentation or take an interactive (needs-satisfaction) approach. The message is intended to persuade buyers to purchase based on the attributes and benefits of the seller's product.

Meeting Objections, part of the presentation process, is an important sales skill. Objections raised by a prospect may represent a request for clarification or additional information. Well-prepared salespeople will anticipate objections and be prepared to overcome them.

Closing the Sale is the stage at which the seller tries to gain a purchase commitment from the prospect. Salespeople who are uncertain that it is an appropriate time to "close the deal" may use a trial close. If a trial close seems to be going well, it can be pursued to a complete close. If not, it can be withdrawn without detracting from the effectiveness of the meeting.

The **Follow-Up** step in the process represents the salesperson's efforts to assure customer satisfaction after the sale. These efforts provide an important basis for building goodwill and future sales. It may also be used to suggest additional sales of the product or related goods.

Canned sales presentations are memorized messages. Salespeople using canned presentations deliver the same prepared statement to each prospect. **Interactive** presentations rely heavily on learning more about each prospect's needs and preferences through direct interaction. Salespeople using this "needs-satisfaction" approach tailor each sales message to each customer. By allowing the potential buyer to speak initially about his or her needs, the salesperson can respond by explaining how the product will address those needs. It is a problem-solving approach to selling. Many salespeople employ parts of both strategies.

Relationship Selling refers to those salesperson's activities that are focused on building ties to the customer. Paying attention to buyer's needs and being truly committed to the customer's satisfaction are the key components of relationship selling.

Partnership Selling refers to formal arrangements between buyers and sellers that create unique, customized products and services for the buyer. This often requires each party to share their unique knowledge and expertise with the other in ways that are not characteristic of conventional buyer-seller relationships. This includes disclosing sensitive competitive and company information, as well as providing access to each other's technical experts.

Sales Force Structure refers to how sellers choose to organize their sales force. A sales force can be organized according to geographic territories, product lines, or customer types. Companies may have both **inside** and **outside** sales forces. Inside salespeople conduct business from their offices via telecommunications media or meet with clients at the seller's location. Outside salespersons travel to make sales calls on customers.

Salesforce Compensation plans may take one of three basic forms: **Straight Salary**, **Straight Commission**, or **A Combination Plan**. The appropriateness of each option is determined by balancing the need to provide income security (salary) versus sales incentives (commission). Combination Plans provide for some measure of both.

The **Drawing Account Method** is a modification of the straight commission plan. Under this method, sales commissions are credited to each individual's drawing account. Salespeople may withdraw a fixed amount each period against their current balance or as an advance against future commissions. In most instances, employees are responsible for any indebtedness incurred under this plan. Some employers, however, provide a **guaranteed draw** where the salesperson is not obligated to pay back the difference when the draw exceeds commissions earned over a specified period.

A great deal of information about the performance of salespeople can be obtained from Sales Reports. Sales Reports describe each individual's schedule of calls and sales results. Key measures of a salesperson's performance include revenue per call, number of calls per day, time per contact, cost per call, percentage of "successes" per call, and the number of new customers created.

Ratios are often used in the **evaluation process**. Among the most common evaluation ratios are Sales/Sales Potential, Sales Expense/Sales, Total Accounts/ Total Potential Number of Accounts, and Total Number of Calls/Number of Accounts. Comparisons may be made to the same salesperson's performance in previous periods or to the performance standards established by others.

Qualitative measures are also used to evaluate salespeople. Customer satisfaction can be measured through telephone interviews or mail questionnaires. Many firms also provide for formal assessment of salespeople's knowledge of the company, its products, customers, and competitors.

SALES PROMOTION

Sales Promotion is comprised of all paid marketing communications other than advertising, public relations, and personal selling. In contrast to advertising, sales promotions are usually intended to provide short-term boosts in product sales. The types of sales promotions typically aimed at final consumers and intermediaries are listed below.

Consumer-Directed—Coupons, Contests, Sweepstakes, Rebates, Premiums, Refunds, Point-of-Purchase Displays, Product Samples, Trading Stamps, Cents-Off Deals, Multi-Pack Offers, Demonstrations, Free Trial Offers.

Intermediary-Directed—Push Money, Trade Allowances, Quantity Discounts, Sales Contests, Trade Shows, Point-of-Purchase Display Materials, Trade Rebates.

DIRECT MARKETING

Direct Marketing refers to one-on-one communications with targeted customers and is aimed primarily at obtaining an immediate response. Direct marketing media include catalogs, direct mail, telemarketing, infomercials, faxes, email, and online Internet services. Companies engaged in direct marketing collect comprehensive data about customers and prospects in electronic databases. These databases typically contain information about prior purchase behavior, demographics, psychographics, and geographic data.

Online Marketing refers to all marketing activities conducted through interactive online computer networks or systems that link buyers and sellers. The Internet is the dominant online marketing channel. **Electronic Commerce** is the term used to describe all forms of buying and selling that is supported by electronic means. The benefits of online marketing to both buyers and sellers are summarized in the table below.

Buyers	Sellers
Convenience (no driving, parking, etc.)	Good tools for building relationships
Private	Opportunity to learn more about buyers
Abundance of Choices (multiple sellers)	Customize product offering to buyer needs
Time Savings	Access to a truly global marketplace
Interactive (site provides info and options)	Reduced costs—increased efficiency
Immediate	Flexible—website is easily changed

8: PRICING POLICIES AND STRATEGIES

PRICE ELASTICITY OF DEMAND

Price elasticity of demand is the percentage change in the number of units demanded divided by the percentage change in the price of the product. It reflects the degree to which the level of product sales is dependent on price. Specifically, it relates the rate at which demand changes in response to price changes. The mathematical formula for price elasticity of demand is shown below.

$$\text{Price Elasticity of Demand} = \frac{(Q_1 - Q_2)/Q_1 + Q_2}{(P_1 - P_2)/P_1 + P_2}$$

Where: Q_1 = Initial Quantity Demanded
Q_2 = New Quantity Demanded
P_1 = Initial Price
P_2 = New Price

Elastic Demand exists when the value of the price elasticity of demand formula is less than -1. If demand is elastic, an increase in price will produce a decrease in demand and a decrease in total revenue. (Total Revenue is the product of price times the number of units sold.) Price decreases will increase demand and **increase** total revenue.

Inelastic Demand exists when the value of the price elasticity of demand formula is greater than -1. If demand is inelastic, an increase in price will produce a decrease in demand and an **increase** in total revenue. Price decreases will increase demand and **decrease** total revenue. If demand does not decrease at all in response to price increases, it is said to be perfectly inelastic.

Unitary Elasticity exists when the value of the price elasticity of demand formula is -1. In this instance, the change in demand is directly proportional to the change in price. When unitary elasticity exists, total revenue does not change in response to price increases or decreases.

The **Price Elasticity of Demand Coefficient (E_d)** is equal to the **absolute value** or non-negative value of the Price Elasticity of Demand formula (shown on the previous page). The interpretation of E_d is provided in the table below.

Value of E_d	Effect of an Increase in Price on Quantity Demanded (Q_d) and Total Revenue (TR)
If E_d = 0 (Perfectly Inelastic)	No Change in Q_d, TR Increases
If E_d < 1 (Inelastic)	Q_d Decreases, TR Increases
If E_d = 1 (Unitary Elasticity)	Q_d Decreases, No Change in TR
If E_d > 1 (Elastic)	Q_d Decreases, TR Decreases
If E_d = ∞ (Perfectly Elastic)	Q_d = 0, TR = 0

The price elasticity of demand for a given product may change significantly at different price levels. Consequently, the value of E_d should be evaluated at several different prices.

PRICE FIXING AND PRICE DISCRIMINATION

The Sherman Act (1890) prevents businesses from restraining trade and interstate commerce. Pricing policies that are predatory or otherwise contribute to the monopolization of markets and conspiracies contrary to competitive pricing are illegal under the provisions of this law.

The Robinson-Patman Act (1936) prohibits any form of price discrimination that has the effect of reducing competition among wholesalers or retailers. The law provides that the same seller cannot provide the same products to competing buyers (resellers) at different prices unless those price differentials can be justified on the basis of cost savings or good faith efforts to meet competitors' prices. The Robinson-Patman Act also prohibits producers from providing a higher level of service to large customers.

PRICING STRATEGY

Price Skimming is a strategy that introduces new products at relatively high prices. Higher initial prices enhance the perceived quality of the product and maintain demand at a level consistent with the firm's production capacity. The higher profit margins may offset some R&D costs and protect the firm from failing to cover costs.

After the initial introductory period, the firm often lowers its price gradually in response to competitive pressures and the need to reach new market segments. In this way the firm can "skim" layers of profitability from each successive price level. Initially, high prices are paid by the least price-sensitive segment of the market. Lowering product prices over time provides the expansion of the market and growth.

Penetration Pricing is an alternative pricing strategy for new product introductions. This option uses low introductory prices to gain a large share of the market more quickly than price skimming would allow. This is especially appropriate for new products that are very similar to competing brands. The lower-price strategy may have several advantages. It provides for quick entry into new markets and often discourages potential competitors from entering. Building relatively high volume sales can also reduce the firm's unit costs through economies of scale. The disadvantages stem from lower unit profit margins and less pricing flexibility.

PRICING DECISIONS

Pricing decisions are often characterized as belonging to one of three categories: cost-based, demand-based, or competition-based pricing. In practice, most pricing decisions integrate elements from each of these categories. Prices typically reflect marketers' consideration of product-related costs, consumer preferences, and competitors' prices.

Cost-Based Pricing establishes product prices as a function of product costs. Cost-based pricing techniques include cost-plus pricing and return-on-investment pricing. Cost-plus pricing determines prices by adding a predetermined level of profit to product costs. Return-on-investment pricing sets product prices that will enable the firm to achieve a specified rate of return. This method requires forecasting sales volume over the life of the investment period. Virtually all price-setting strategies must take costs into account as part of the process.

Demand-Based Pricing attempts to set prices based on consumer responses to product prices. Demand-based pricing techniques include prestige pricing, odd-even pricing, price lining, and leader pricing. These methods of setting prices are sometimes referred to as psychological pricing. Market research on consumer attitudes and preferences often identify the range of acceptable prices specific to each market segment.

Competition-Based Pricing sets prices according to those charged by the firm's closest competitors. This may result in prices above, below, or at market levels. Competition-based pricing strategies include customary pricing and price leadership. In certain markets, competitors have converged on a narrow range of price points. This traditional basis for setting prices is referred to as Customary Pricing. Price Leadership exists when one firm is usually the first to change prices from previous levels and this change is routinely followed by the rest of the industry.

A **One-Price** policy offers the same price to all buyers for purchases of essentially the same quantities in comparable situations. **Flexible Pricing** permits the seller to charge different prices to different buyers in similar circumstances. This strategy is most common in personal selling contexts. Flexible pricing allows the salesperson to adjust prices in response to competitive shifts and customer requirements.

Geographic Pricing policies reflect different levels of transportation and other costs related to the physical distance between buyers and sellers. Sellers may quote F.O.B. (free-on-board) prices, which do not include shipping charges. Zone pricing sets separate prices for different geographic regions— incorporating average transport costs for each area into the quoted prices of the product.

Unit Pricing provides consumers with information on the price per unit on or near the product. This practice is intended to simplify comparisons between brands and various package sizes.

With **alternative pricing objectives**, a firm's pricing strategy may reflect short-term goals other than profit maximization. Short-term price reductions may be intended to build market share, build brand awareness in a new market or segment, change customers' perceptions of product value, move inventory, gain distributor acceptance, or accelerate the pace of new product adoption.

PRICE-QUALITY CORRELATION

In many instances, consumers believe that higher prices represent superior product quality. In the absence of specific product information, buyers often rely on price as an indicator of quality and use this measure when evaluating brands. This price-quality correlation is strongest when buyers have little confidence in their ability to judge product quality and they suspect substantial differences in quality between brands.

PSYCHOLOGICAL PRICING

Prestige Pricing establishes retail prices that are high, relative to competing brands. The higher price is intended to suggest higher product quality, consistent with the strength of the price-quality association in consumers' minds. It may also provide the product with a measure of prestige or status relative to competing brands.

Odd-Even Pricing sets prices just below even dollar values (e.g., $99.99 or $99 v. $100). There are several possible explanations for consumers' apparent preference for certain odd prices, rather than even ones. Buyers may implicitly believe that odd prices are the consequence of a price reduction from a higher even price. They may prefer odd prices because they seem substantially lower (the difference between $100 and $99 seems far more than one dollar). It may also provide shoppers with a reference point when trying to stay within price limits. On balance, consumers seem to feel that odd prices provide greater value for their money.

Consumers may also seek "even" prices under some circumstances. When prices for a product category (e.g., candy bars, chewing gum) have remained relatively stable over extended periods, buyers may have very adverse reactions to any increase. When confronted with rising costs, marketers may try to maintain these **customary prices** by reducing the size of each package or changing the ingredients used in production.

Price Lining simplifies consumers' evaluation of alternative products by establishing a limited number of price points for groups or lines of products. Product groups of similar quality are all sold at the same price, thereby allowing shoppers to evaluate alternatives based on other considerations. A retailer may, for example, price various styles and lines of shirts at three price levels: $24, $29, and $36.

When establishing a price line, the seller must be certain that price points are far enough apart so that buyers perceive different levels of merchandise quality. Price lining may minimize consumers' confusion when comparing brands while allowing retailers to maintain a wider assortment within specified price ranges.

Leader Pricing occurs when a firm sells select products below their usual price as a means of gaining attention or building store traffic. In retail settings, leader pricing tends to feature popular brands of frequently purchased products. The expectation is that sales of regularly priced merchandise will benefit from increased traffic and that the image of the store as a price leader will be enhanced. When items are sold below cost, they are termed "loss leaders."

PROFIT MARGIN

Markups are percentages or dollar amounts added to the cost of sales to arrive at the product's selling price. Many retailers and wholesalers use a standard percentage markup to set selling prices. Markups are usually calculated as a percentage of the selling price, rather than a percentage of the cost.

$$\text{Markup Percentage (On Selling Price)} = \frac{\text{Selling Price} - \text{Product Cost}}{\text{Selling Price}}$$

Example: Product Cost = $50 Selling Price = $80

$$\text{Markup Percentage} = \frac{\$80 - \$50}{\$80} = \frac{\$30}{\$80} = .375 \text{ or } 37.5\%$$
(On Selling Price)

$$\text{Selling Price} = \text{Markup Amount} + \text{Product Cost}$$
(to find Markup Amount: Product Cost × Markup Percent)

Example: Product Cost = $30 Markup Percentage = 60%
Markup Amount = $30 × .6 = $18
Selling Price = $18 + $30 = $48

Markdowns are retail price reductions. Managers typically markdown retail prices in response to low consumer demand. Like markups, mark-downs are usually expressed as a percentage of the selling price.

$$\text{Markup Percentage (On Selling Price)} = \frac{\text{Original Selling Price} - \text{Reduced Price}}{\text{Original Selling Price}}$$

Example: Product Cost = $50 Selling Price = $80

$$\text{Markup Percentage (On Selling Price)} = \frac{\$85 - \$60}{\$85} = .294 \text{ or } 29.4\%$$

Discounts are reductions from list prices that are given by sellers to buyers. These price reductions may be based on several factors.

Trade Discounts are reductions from the list price given to intermediaries in exchange for the performance of specified tasks. Trade discounts may compensate buyers for promotional considerations, transportation, storage costs, extending credit, and order processing.

Quantity Discounts arise from the economies and improved efficiency of selling in large quantities. As order size increases, the fixed costs related to order processing and customer service remain substantially unchanged. Consequently, the associated per unit costs are reduced for the seller. In turn, some financing and storage costs may also be shifted to the buyer. Quantity discounts may be cumulative over a specified period of time or noncumulative.

Cash Discounts are given to encourage buyers to provide payment promptly. For example, 2/10 net 30 is a common policy that gives buyers a two percent discount if the account is paid within 10 days. "Net 30" indicates that the balance is due within 30 days. If the account is not paid within 30 days, interest may be charged.

Seasonal Discounts are used to encourage buyers to make their purchases off-season. This strategy may provide needed cash to the seller, reduce inventories, or help to smooth out production scheduling.

Allowances are price reductions that are intended to achieve specific goals. Trade-in allowances may make financing a purchase easier for the buyer. Promotional allowances are used to secure reseller participation in advertising and sales support programs intended to boost product sales.

Break-Even Analysis allows managers to estimate the impact of alternative price levels on profits. The Break-Even Point is the price at which total revenue just equals total costs. When sales exceed the break-even level for a given price, each successive unit sold generates profit.

> **Total Revenue = Price × Quantity Sold**
>
> **Total Costs = Fixed Costs + (Variables Cost per Unit × Quantity Sold)**
>
> $$\text{Break-Even Point (Units)} = \frac{\text{Total Fixed Costs}}{\text{Price} - \text{Variable Cost Per Unit}}$$

Each price level has its own break-even point. The value of break-even analysis stems from its usefulness in evaluating pricing options. It should not, however, be relied on as the sole basis for setting prices. The assumptions implicit in using straight line total revenue and total cost curves are not realistic. If they were, profits would continue to grow indefinitely once the break-even point was surpassed. Break-even analysis represents one additional perspective on price setting that should be incorporated with other cost-based, demand-based, and competition-based pricing strategies.

9: SPECIAL TOPICS IN MARKETING

INTERNATIONAL MARKETING

Any firm that markets products outside its own country is engaged in international marketing. The essentials of marketing are applicable throughout the world. Success in international marketing is contingent on creating a marketing mix that matches the needs and preferences of the target market. The complexity of international marketing operations stems from the need to understand differences between countries and cultures. Among the cultural differences that may impact the marketing plan of a firm are language, family structure, social customs, religion, and educational systems. Government policies may also pose substantial barriers to trade with other countries.

There are several types of intermediaries that can be used to enter foreign markets. Firms may engage the services of import-export intermediaries who provide expertise in international operations. This option requires very little investment on the part of the exporter. Firms willing to commit more resources to international ventures may establish company-owned sales branches in foreign countries. Firms committed to operations in a foreign country may establish wholly-owned foreign subsidiaries.

NONPROFIT MARKETING

Marketing principles and practices are applied within a wide range of nonprofit organizations. Nonprofit marketing applications include the marketing of **Persons**, **Ideas**, and **Organizations**. In contrast to business firms, nonprofit organizations pursue nonfinancial, social, and service objectives. They also differ from "for-profit" ventures by their need to attract volunteer labor and financial contributions. Consequently, nonprofit groups need to satisfy two distinct target markets: donors/supporters and clients/recipients of their services. In addition, their objectives often include gaining the approval and support of society at-large for their causes as well as their organizations.

HISTORY OF THE MARKETING CONCEPT

The Production Era. Beginning in the second half of the nineteenth century, electricity, rail transportation, division of labor, assembly lines, and other mass production concepts made it possible to manufacture goods more efficiently. The prevailing business philosophy of the era emphasized economies of scale in production, improved efficiency, cost containment, and the principles of scientific management.

The Sales Era. From the mid-1920s through the 1950s, the emphasis of the prevailing business philosophy was on sales as the primary means of increasing profits. Personal selling and advertising were regarded as the most important marketing functions.

The Marketing Era. By the early 1950s, many businesses recognized that efficient production and extensive promotion did not guarantee that customers would buy what was being sold. Businesses turned their attention to understanding and serving customers' needs. This emphasis on customer satisfaction resulted in increased concerns about ethics and social responsibility.

THE ROLE OF MARKETING IN THE ECONOMY

Individuals and organizations engage in marketing activities to facilitate exchanges. For an exchange to take place, these four conditions must exist:

1. Two or more individuals or organizations must participate
2. Each party must possess something of value that the other wants to acquire
3. Each party must be willing to give up something of value to acquire something of value
4. Both parties must be able to communicate with each other

In the end, exchanges should satisfy both buyer and seller.

Marketing activities help promote exchanges and produce the profits that are essential to the survival of individual companies and the overall health of the economy. Approximately one-half of buyers' expenditures on products go to cover marketing-related costs.

MARKETING ETHICS

Marketing Ethics are the moral principles that define right and wrong behavior in marketing practice. Many organizations formalize rules and standards of ethical conduct that define what is expected of their employees. These

codes of conduct are intended to eliminate opportunities for unethical behavior that will reflect badly on the organization.

Ethical models of marketing behavior can be either **compensatory** or **non-compensatory** in nature. Compensatory models are those where the moral right or wrong of an action is determined by the consequences the action produces. "Right action is that which maximizes the good." Noncompensatory models are those that maintain a universally true moral principle with no exceptions. These rules do not allow for considering the consequences of an act. These ethical rules have three tenets: no exceptions to the rule; the principle is impartial; and, it must be consistently applied.

Social Responsibility refers to the firm's obligations to society. Social responsibility has four dimensions: economic, legal, ethical, and philanthropic. The ideal for a socially responsible organization is to maximize the positive impacts and minimize the negative impacts of the firm, while it is operating within its own best interests.

Green Marketing refers to the design, development, and marketing of products that do not harm the environment. Green Marketing initiatives emphasize efforts to reduce or eliminate waste in the production and distribution of products. **Reverse logistics** is a concept that emphasizes the responsibility of the firm for products after they are disposed of by consumers. Recycling and salvaging usable materials from discarded products is a key concept in reverse logistics.

PART III

Practice Tests

PRACTICE TEST 1

CLEP Principles of Marketing

Also available at the REA Study Center (*www.rea.com/studycenter*)

This practice test is also offered online at the REA Study Center. Since all CLEP exams are administered on computer, we recommend that you take the online version of this test to simulate test-day conditions and to receive these added benefits:

- **Timed testing conditions** – helps you gauge how much time you can spend on each question
- **Automatic scoring** – find out how you did on the test, instantly
- **On-screen detailed explanations of answers** – gives you the correct answer and explains why the other answer choices are wrong
- **Diagnostic score reports** – pinpoint where you're strongest and where you need to focus your study

PRACTICE TEST 1

CLEP Principles of Marketing

(Answer sheets appear in the back of the book.)

TIME: 90 Minutes
100 Questions

DIRECTIONS: Each of the questions or incomplete statements below is followed by five possible answers or completions. Select the best choice in each case and fill in the corresponding oval on the answer sheet.

1. The production of a new car model includes which of the following activities?

   (A) Predicting the types of cars different types of people will buy
   (B) Actually making the car
   (C) Determining the features of the car
   (D) Selling the car
   (E) Developing a sales promotion campaign for the car

2. The term "micro-macro dilemma" means that

   (A) people have a hard time making choices between products
   (B) every economy needs a macro-marketing system but not necessarily a micro-marketing system
   (C) what is good for some producers may not be good for society as a whole
   (D) satisfying a customer's wants and needs is difficult because the consumer may not know what his/her wants and needs are
   (E) it is difficult to determine consumer tastes in the globally diverse marketplace

3. An organized way of continually gathering and analyzing data to provide marketing managers with the most up-to-date information they need to make decisions is called

   (A) decision support systems (DSS)
   (B) time series models
   (C) marketing research
   (D) marketing information systems (MIS)
   (E) consumer panels

4. Ogden Parts Inc. has named a new sales manager with responsibilities for market planning. Ogden's president thinks the sales manager should sell more parts and outsell the competition. It seems that this company is run as if it were in the

   (A) sales era
   (B) production era
   (C) marketing company era
   (D) simple trade era
   (E) marketing department era

5. The "four P's" of a marketing mix are

   (A) Product, Price, Profit, Promotion
   (B) People, Product, Place, Promotion
   (C) Promotion, Production, Price, Place
   (D) Product, Price, Place, Promotion
   (E) Profit, Place, Price, Product

6. The role of price in a market-directed economy is to

   (A) determine the sale prices of clearance items in a retail store
   (B) serve as a rough measure of the value of resources used to produce goods and services
   (C) ensure no consumer pays prices that are too high
   (D) determine the amount of losses that can be sustained by a company
   (E) allocate profits to companies even though they may not be providing the most desirable goods and services

7. Which of the following statements about marketing is FALSE?

    (A) Marketing attempts to affect the products and services you buy.
    (B) Marketing does not apply to nonprofit organizations.
    (C) Advertising and sales promotion are marketing functions.
    (D) Marketing can affect the prices you will pay for a product.
    (E) Marketing includes decisions about how to sell products.

8. Family units in Smallisland Country make all the products they consume. This is an example of

    (A) an economy where marketing is efficient
    (B) a pure market-oriented economy
    (C) a planned economy
    (D) an economy where the role of middlemen is important
    (E) a pure subsistence economy

9. Tariffs are

    (A) taxes on imported products
    (B) predetermined prices planned by several competing companies
    (C) rules on the amount of products that can be imported
    (D) extra money paid to officials for favored status
    (E) illegal in the United States

10. As XYZ Company produces larger quantities of watches, the cost of producing each watch goes down. This is known as

    (A) micro-marketing
    (B) possession utility
    (C) economies of scale
    (D) marketing concept
    (E) transaction efficiency

11. The Magnuson Act of 1975 says that

    (A) producers of goods must warrant their products as merchantable
    (B) a written warranty reduces the responsibility of a producer
    (C) producers must provide a clearly written warranty
    (D) each product must be identified with a readable electronic code
    (E) goods must be clearly labeled and easy to understand

12. When marketers focus on comparing their product versus a competitor's product, they

    (A) formulate a SWOT analysis
    (B) should be concerned with total product offering
    (C) look at the relative quality
    (D) Both (B) and (C)
    (E) All of the above

13. One would consider an intangible deed performed by one party for another party at a cost as a

    (A) supply
    (B) service
    (C) good
    (D) perishable good
    (E) Both (B) and (D)

14. Which of the following is NOT true about the three types of convenience products (staples, impulse products, and emergency products)?

    (A) Staples are products that are bought routinely, without much thought.
    (B) With impulse products, much of the buyer's behavior affects place utility.
    (C) Customers shop extensively when purchasing these items.
    (D) Emergency products are purchased when urgently needed.
    (E) With staples, branding helps customers cut shopping efforts.

15. New product planning is becoming increasingly important in a modern economy because

    (A) most profits go to innovators or fast companies that quickly copy products from other companies
    (B) it is not always profitable *just* to sell "me-too" products
    (C) the failure rate of new products is becoming increasingly low
    (D) every product must pass FTC laws to be bought and sold
    (E) All of the above are true

16. A capital item (a necessary element in setting price) is best described as

    (A) a building or other type of major equipment
    (B) office supplies purchased by the individuals
    (C) raw materials that become part of the physical good
    (D) long-lasting products that can be depreciated
    (E) Both (A) and (D)

17. Which of the following symbols is a trademark?

    (A)

    (B)

    (C)

    (D) All of the above
    (E) None of the above

18. The practice of tailoring products and marketing programs to suit the needs of specific individuals is called

    (A) niche marketing
    (B) mass marketing
    (C) segment marketing
    (D) micro-marketing
    (E) macro-marketing

19. Packaging is of importance to marketers because

    (A) it provides better shelf placement in grocery stores
    (B) packaging costs over 95% of a manufacturer's selling price
    (C) the Federal Packaging and Labeling Act holds restrictions on packaging sizes
    (D) new packages can make a difference in a new marketing strategy
    (E) labels are inaccurate, and no one reads them anyway

20. What level of familiarity exists when a consumer buys paper clips for the office, and she/he does not notice the brand name of the product?

    (A) Brand rejection
    (B) Brand recognition
    (C) Brand nonrecognition
    (D) Brand preference
    (E) Brand insistence

21. Some customers feel that certain brands of refrigerators are very similar and have the same attributes. By shopping for the best price, or lowest price, what kinds of products are these?

    (A) Specialty products
    (B) Heterogeneous products
    (C) Convenience products
    (D) Regularly sought products
    (E) Homogeneous products

22. When Progresso makes Cajun gumbo soup for Louisiana and nacho cheese soup for Texas, what kind of segmentation is it practicing?

    (A) Geographic
    (B) Behavioral
    (C) Demographic
    (D) Psychographic
    (E) Political

23. Which of the following statements is NOT true about the product life cycle?

    (A) As industry sales rise, industry profits also rise.
    (B) Each stage may have a different target market.
    (C) In general, competition tends to move toward pure competition.
    (D) Industry profits start to decrease in market growth.
    (E) Both (A) and (D)

24. Which statement is correct about the market growth stage?

    (A) Industry profits tend to increase in the beginning of the stage.
    (B) Industry profits decrease toward the end of the stage.
    (C) More companies enter the industry.
    (D) Industry sales increase.
    (E) All the above are correct statements.

25. All of the following would be ways to segment a market within the category of "psychographic segmentation" EXCEPT

    (A) social class
    (B) personality
    (C) occupation
    (D) lifestyle
    (E) interests

26. All of the following are considered to be major variables for segmenting markets EXCEPT

    (A) geographic
    (B) demographic
    (C) behavioral
    (D) moods
    (E) psychographic

27. Mingilton Meats increased the price of their bologna from $2.00 a pound to $3.00 a pound. After doing this they noticed a decrease in total revenue. This is because

    (A) the demand for the meat is elastic
    (B) the demand for the meat is inelastic
    (C) the demand is unitarily elastic
    (D) the meat was too old to purchase
    (E) Cannot tell from the information given

28. The Yearous Group saw an increase in total revenue when the company decreased the price of its golf bags. The marketing manager can assume that the demand is

    (A) unitarily elastic
    (B) elastic
    (C) inelastic
    (D) All of the above
    (E) None of the above

29. A potato farmer in Alamosa, Colorado, would be likely to have which type of demand for his potato crop?

    (A) Inelastic demand
    (B) No demand; everyone buys potatoes from Idaho
    (C) Elastic demand
    (D) Unitary elasticity of demand
    (E) All of the above

30. Bob opened a new restaurant featuring "Crab Legs à la Bob." As he experimented with the price of the offering, he found that no matter if he raised or lowered his price, the total revenue from the "Crab Legs à la Bob" stayed the same. He could conclude that his product had what kind of elasticity?

    (A) He can draw no conclusions from the information given.
    (B) His demand is elastic.
    (C) His demand is inelastic.
    (D) He has a situation where there is unitary elasticity.
    (E) He should sell shrimp.

31. Given the standard commission used in advertising agencies, what would an agency receive for a magazine ad that cost $20,000?

    (A) $1,500
    (B) $1,750
    (C) $2,000
    (D) $3,000
    (E) $5,000

32. Given the following choices, which is NOT considered a retailing activity?

    (A) The Alpha Kappa Psi Fraternity sells coffee to faculty members in the morning at a local college.
    (B) Because your car broke down, you are forced to call a tow truck to tow your car to be fixed, for which you are charged $50.
    (C) A soap company salesperson comes to your door and sells you $10 worth of soap.
    (D) You purchase a new suit at Macy's Department Store for $259.
    (E) All of the above are examples of retailing.

33. If a firm were to obtain information about light, medium, and heavy users of a product as a means to segment their market, the firm would be practicing what kind of segmentation?

    (A) Geographic
    (B) Behavioral
    (C) Demographic
    (D) Psychographic
    (E) Geodemographic

34. Positioning is

    (A) giving a product meaning that distinguishes it from its competition
    (B) occupying a specific place in consumers minds relative to competing products
    (C) not as important as segmentation
    (D) primarily meant for large multinational companies
    (E) Both (A) and (B) are true

35. Disposable diapers, which are not biodegradable, are what type of new product opportunity?

    (A) Desirable products
    (B) Pleasing products
    (C) Performance products
    (D) Deficient products
    (E) Salutary products

36. Which of the following statements could occur in market maturity?

    (A) Industry sales become stable.
    (B) Profits can increase for an individual company.
    (C) Individual firms drop out of the industry.
    (D) Promotion costs rise.
    (E) All of the above

37. Stetson's use of the American cowboy in its advertising is an example of a positioning strategy based on

    (A) a product attribute
    (B) the product's users
    (C) a cultural icon
    (D) against competition
    (E) a product benefit

38. John Randall is a purchasing agent for a rather large delivery service. John has just agreed to purchase a 1992 Chevy van from his brother's construction company, although he has never driven it or seen it. This buying approach would be an example of

    (A) description buying
    (B) test buying
    (C) inspection buying
    (D) sampling buying
    (E) negotiated contract buying

39. Which of the following is NOT part of the Multiple Buying Influence, when making a decision to buy a new copy machine in a business?

    (A) General public
    (B) Influencer
    (C) Buyer
    (D) Decider
    (E) Gatekeeper

40. By definition, "Price" is

    (A) the sticker on a product that suggests a price
    (B) what is charged for something (product or service)
    (C) calculated by dividing cost with retail selling price
    (D) the term used by marketers defining the cost of a product
    (E) profit-oriented

41. Sally Rudolph is selling a new shirt, which she made, to her friend for $1,000. The shirt cost Sally $400. What is her markup?

    (A) $40
    (B) $100
    (C) $300
    (D) $400
    (E) $600

    1,000 − 400

42. If Bob Peters sells a set of steak knives for $1,000, and he has a markup (or selling price) of $600, what is his markup percent?

    (A) 10%
    (B) 20%
    (C) 50%
    (D) 60%
    (E) Cannot be determined from the information given

    60 / 1000 = .6

43. What is the retail price if the cost of a product is $400, and the markup percent on the retail selling price is 60%?

    (A) $1,000
    (B) $2,000
    (C) $450
    (D) $550
    (E) $600

44. Ron and Dee own a floor tile retail outlet. They want to achieve a 40% markup at retail for all of the merchandise that they sell. If one style of floor tile retails at $3 per tile, what is the maximum that Ron and Dee can pay for the tile?

    (A) $2.06
    (B) $2.10
    (C) $2.14
    (D) $2.22
    (E) Cannot be determined from the information given

    3 + .4

45. Pake Productions wants to mark down a new line of stereo speakers that they have in the stores. After the speakers are marked down, Pake Productions wants to calculate the markdown percentage. If the original price of the speakers was $200, and the new price of the speakers is $160, what is the markdown percent?

    (A) $40
    (B) $50
    (C) 25%
    (D) 20%
    (E) Both (C) and (D) are correct.

46. Ogden & Ogden receive an invoice for $100, which they pay in nine days. The terms on the invoice indicate 2/10 net 30. How much money did Ogden & Ogden send to the seller?

    (A) $100
    (B) $98
    (C) $102
    (D) $2.00
    (E) $96.45

47. Making goods and services available in the right quantities and locations when the customer wants them is the definition for which one of the following marketing mix variables?

    (A) Promotion
    (B) Place
    (C) Product
    (D) Price
    (E) None of the above

48. Alarid Company purchases goods from a manufacturer who then turns around and sells them to a retailer who sells them to final customers. The Alarid Company is participating in a(n)

    (A) regrouping activity
    (B) accumulating activity
    (C) channel of distribution
    (D) bulk-breaking project
    (E) None of the above

49. In terms of direct marketing expenses, the second biggest category after telemarketing is

    (A) radio direct response
    (B) television infomercials
    (C) direct mail
    (D) magazine direct marketing
    (E) Internet marketing

50. Which of the following is an important advantage of direct marketing?

    (A) Low cost
    (B) Ability to tailor messages to a specific audience
    (C) Fast response time between placing and shipping the order
    (D) Ability to use just-in-time inventory management
    (E) High rate of consumer acceptance

51. ABC Corporation sells only to wholesalers who give their product special attention. ABC Corporation is practicing what type of distribution?

    (A) Selective distribution
    (B) Intensive distribution
    (C) Exclusive distribution
    (D) Ideal market exposure
    (E) None of the above

52. Public relations firms are often evaluated by the number of "hits" they obtain. A "hit" is

    (A) an advertisement that is successful
    (B) a special event tie-in with publicity
    (C) the mention of a company's name in a news story
    (D) a media story that speaks positively about a company
    (E) a media story that speaks negatively about a company

53. Turner Corporation sells its product to several competing channels that will reach the same target market. Turner Corporation is using what type of distribution?

    (A) Exclusive distribution
    (B) Intensive distribution
    (C) Dual distribution
    (D) Both (A) and (B).
    (E) None of the above

54. Which statement best describes why Dual Distribution is becoming more common with producers and retailers?

    (A) It is best applicable for convenience products and business suppliers.
    (B) Retailers want large quantities with a lower price per unit.
    (C) Present channel members are doing an excellent job.
    (D) Both (A) and (C).
    (E) All of the above

55. The public relations tool that is mostly internally oriented is the

    (A) press release
    (B) company newsletter
    (C) financial statement
    (D) network television spot
    (E) balance of payments statement

56. What are the two basic types of conflicts in channels of distribution?

    (A) Horizontal and vertical
    (B) Discrepancy of quantity and assortment
    (C) Assorting and sorting
    (D) Both (B) and (C)
    (E) None of the above

57. Within the industrial mix, the product variable places a great deal of emphasis on

    (A) price
    (B) services
    (C) environmental influences
    (D) distribution
    (E) sales promotion

58. In regard to industrial marketing, the following example best exemplifies what type of pricing? "The seller determines the price (or a series of prices) for a given product, and the customer pays that specified price."

    (A) Bid pricing
    (B) Negotiated pricing
    (C) Administered pricing
    (D) Retail pricing
    (E) Economic pricing

59. A "perceptual map" is a marketing tool that helps managers with

    (A) positioning decisions
    (B) product design
    (C) packaging decisions
    (D) deciding where in the country to sell a product
    (E) determining shipping costs

60. Advertising can make industrial customers aware of

    (A) new products or brands
    (B) product features
    (C) organizations
    (D) representatives
    (E) All of the above

61. Which of the following statements is NOT true when developing a marketing strategy?

    (A) It allows flexibility in providing for customer service.
    (B) It allows the hiring of high-quality personnel.
    (C) It may help to resolve problems in regard to service.
    (D) It provides for the use of high technology, allowing for lower cost services.
    (E) None of the above.

62. If an organization is conducting marketing activities other than for the goals of profit, market share, or return on investment (ROI), these marketing activities are referred to as

(A) a waste of time
(B) nonbusiness marketing
(C) strategic marketing
(D) promotional marketing
(E) nonmarketing activities

63. Generally speaking, a department store salesperson who stands behind a counter and performs a cashier's role can be classified as a(n)

(A) order getter
(B) order taker
(C) public relations specialist
(D) missionary salesperson
(E) copywriter

64. What is the key to creating value and customer satisfaction?

(A) Total quality
(B) Everyday low prices
(C) Manufacturing superiority
(D) Celebrity advertising
(E) Sales promotions

65. Which of the following choices is NOT a level in the hierarchy of needs?

(A) Money needs
(B) Safety needs
(C) Physiological needs
(D) Social needs
(E) All of the above are levels in the hierarchy of needs.

66. Which of the following choices best defines a change in a person's thought process caused by prior experience?

(A) Cue
(B) Response
(C) Learning
(D) Belief
(E) Reinforcement

67. In marketing, an analysis of a person's day-to-day patterns of living is referred to as a person's AIOs, which are also known as

    (A) Awareness, Interests, Opinions
    (B) Activities, Interests, Opinions
    (C) Actions, Incentives, Objections
    (D) Actions, Integrity, Observations
    (E) Awareness, Incentives, Observations

68. The American market is changing and therefore businesses must adapt to these changes. Today, most successful companies are moving away from

    (A) target marketing
    (B) market segmentation
    (C) market positioning
    (D) mass marketing
    (E) direct marketing

69. Carefully arranging for a product or service to occupy a clear, distinctive, and desirable place relative to competing products or services in the minds of target consumers is called

    (A) mass marketing
    (B) target marketing
    (C) market segmentation
    (D) green marketing
    (E) positioning

70. Which of the following is the best example of a product a consumer would consider under the extensive problem-solving process?

    (A) Milk
    (B) Washing machine
    (C) Pair of shoes
    (D) Toilet paper
    (E) T-shirt

71. Which of the following is NOT one of the steps in the adoption process?

    (A) Confirmation
    (B) Trial
    (C) Awareness
    (D) Decision
    (E) Payment

72. Which of the following is NOT a function of channels of distribution?

    (A) Alleviating discrepancies in assortment
    (B) Alleviating discrepancies in quantity
    (C) Providing customer service
    (D) New product development
    (E) Creating utility

73. Which of the following is NOT a regrouping activity used by channel specialists to adjust discrepancies?

    (A) Assorting
    (B) Accumulating
    (C) Transforming
    (D) Bulk-Breaking
    (E) Sorting

74. Which of the following is one of the reasons that personal selling can be more effective than advertising in a complex selling situation?

    (A) Personal selling is cheaper on a per contact basis.
    (B) Personal selling can reach more customers within a given time period.
    (C) Personal selling can deal with inelastic demand.
    (D) Personal selling can probe customers to learn more about their needs.
    (E) Only (A) and (B) are true.

75. The combining of two or more stages of the channel under one management, in which each channel member is seen as an extension of their own operations, is described as

    (A) strategic alliances
    (B) horizontal channel integration
    (C) reverse channels
    (D) oligopoly
    (E) vertical channel integration

76. Which type of distribution would best be used for products such as soap, food, and personal care products when consumers desire wide availability of the products?

   (A) Intensive distribution
   (B) Exclusive distribution
   (C) Vertical distribution
   (D) Horizontal distribution
   (E) Selective distribution

77. Which type of distribution technique used a single outlet in a fairly large geographic area to distribute a product or service such as Jaguar and Rolls-Royce automobiles?

   (A) Selective
   (B) Universal
   (C) Intensive
   (D) Exclusive
   (E) None of the above

78. A major reason why some shoppers are reluctant to make Internet purchases is because of

   (A) higher prices
   (B) inferior quality
   (C) concern about security
   (D) greater inconvenience
   (E) poor selection

79. Forbidding an intermediary to carry products of a competing manufacturer is known as

   (A) tying agreement
   (B) monopoly
   (C) exclusive dealing
   (D) strategic channel alliance
   (E) vertical marketing system

80. A coupon on a bottle of Pepsi offering a deal on a bag of potato chips is called

    (A) cross-ruff coupon
    (B) scanner-delivered coupon
    (C) instant redemption coupon
    (D) response offer coupon
    (E) bounce back coupon

81. Which of the following is the most widely used positioning strategy?

    (A) Against a competitor
    (B) Away from a competitor
    (C) Product attribute
    (D) User's lifestyle
    (E) User's occupation

82. Which of the following factors is at the core of the marketing concept?

    (A) Mass marketing
    (B) Aggressive selling
    (C) Brand preference
    (D) Low prices
    (E) Customer satisfaction

83. The strategy of choosing one attribute to excel at or to create competitive advantage is called

    (A) overpositioning
    (B) unique selling proposition
    (C) undifferentiated marketing
    (D) relationship marketing
    (E) concentrated marketing

84. Which of the following pricing policies seems to be the one favored by e-commerce and Internet-based businesses?

    (A) Complementary pricing policies
    (B) Dynamic pricing policies
    (C) Standard pricing policies
    (D) Fixed pricing policies
    (E) Prestige pricing

85. Which of the following choices is an example of a manufacturer's brand?

    (A) Heinz ketchup
    (B) Diehard batteries
    (C) Craftsman tools
    (D) Kenmore appliances
    (E) All of the above

86. A strategy that consists of the seller's development of two or more brands in the same product category is called

    (A) brand repositioning decision
    (B) brand extension decision
    (C) multibrand decision
    (D) family brand decision
    (E) brand quality decision

87. Setting prices as low as possible typically supports which of the following pricing objectives?

    (A) Market share leadership
    (B) Product quality leadership
    (C) Current profit maximization
    (D) Survival
    (E) Just-in-time policy

88. Rent, heating and air-conditioning, interest, and executive salaries would all be examples of

    (A) standard costs
    (B) variable costs
    (C) fixed costs
    (D) independent costs
    (E) monopoly costs

89. Which of the following statements is NOT a reason for downward stretching the product line?

 (A) The company is attacked at the high end and decides to counterattack by invading the low end.
 (B) The company finds that slower growth is taking place at the high end.
 (C) The company at the lower end of the market may want to enter the higher end.
 (D) The company initially entered the high end to establish a quality image and intended to roll downward.
 (E) The company adds a low-end unit to plug a market hole that would otherwise attract a new competitor.

90. The most important factor pushing marketers toward integrated marketing communication is

 (A) increasing competition
 (B) decreasing costs of advertising
 (C) declining use of sales promotions
 (D) spiraling costs of personal selling
 (E) increased reliance on one medium of advertising

91. Electronic monitoring systems that link consumers' exposure to TV advertising (measured using television meters) with what they actually buy in stores (measured by store checkout scanners) are called

 (A) motivational research systems
 (B) single-source data systems
 (C) peoplemeters
 (D) subliminal research systems
 (E) focus group data

92. The two major economic factors that reflect a country's attractiveness as an export market are

 (A) industrial structure and income distribution
 (B) political stability and attitudes
 (C) cultural environment and government bureaucracy
 (D) joint venturing and direct investment
 (E) contract manufacturing and management contracting

93. Which of the following economies creates a new rich class and a small, but growing, middle-class that both demand new types of imported goods?

(A) Subsistence economy
(B) Raw-material-exporting economy
(C) Industrialized economy
(D) Industrializing economy
(E) None of the above.

94. Whenever possible, smart marketers will take a _____ rather than _____ aproach to the marketing environment. (Choose the best combination from the options below.)

(A) reactive .. proactive
(B) proactive .. reactive
(C) offensive .. defensive
(D) defensive .. offensive
(E) overt .. covert

95. The simplest way to enter a foreign market is through

(A) joint venturing
(B) licensing
(C) management contracting
(D) direct investment
(E) exporting

96. Marketing a product in a foreign market without any change to the product is called

(A) straight extension
(B) product adaptation
(C) product invention
(D) communication adaptation
(E) dual adaptation

97. Which form of entry into a foreign market causes the most risk?

(A) Exporting
(B) Joint venturing
(C) Joint ownership
(D) Licensing
(E) Direct investment

98. Which type of joint venturing offers a low-risk method of getting into a foreign market and yields income from the beginning?

    (A) Licensing
    (B) Contract manufacturing
    (C) Management contracting
    (D) Joint ownership
    (E) Both (A) and (B) are correct.

99. With the high regulation of the U.S. government before the 1980s, carriers of products did not compete in which of these areas, as they do now?

    (A) Promotion
    (B) Price
    (C) Place
    (D) Product
    (E) Service

100. Sandy just bought a new Ford Taurus. Three weeks later, she received a rebate check for $300 in the mail. Which of the following forms of promotion was used in this example?

    (A) Advertising
    (B) Direct marketing
    (C) Sales promotion
    (D) Personal selling
    (E) Public relations

PRACTICE TEST 1

Answer Key

1.	(B)	35.	(B)	69.	(E)
2.	(C)	36.	(E)	70.	(B)
3.	(D)	37.	(C)	71.	(E)
4.	(A)	38.	(A)	72.	(D)
5.	(D)	39.	(A)	73.	(C)
6.	(B)	40.	(B)	74.	(D)
7.	(B)	41.	(E)	75.	(E)
8.	(E)	42.	(D)	76.	(A)
9.	(A)	43.	(A)	77.	(D)
10.	(C)	44.	(C)	78.	(C)
11.	(C)	45.	(E)	79.	(C)
12.	(D)	46.	(B)	80.	(A)
13.	(B)	47.	(B)	81.	(C)
14.	(C)	48.	(C)	82.	(E)
15.	(B)	49.	(C)	83.	(B)
16.	(E)	50.	(B)	84.	(B)
17.	(D)	51.	(A)	85.	(A)
18.	(D)	52.	(C)	86.	(C)
19.	(D)	53.	(C)	87.	(C)
20.	(C)	54.	(B)	88.	(C)
21.	(E)	55.	(B)	89.	(C)
22.	(A)	56.	(A)	90.	(A)
23.	(A)	57.	(B)	91.	(B)
24.	(E)	58.	(C)	92.	(A)
25.	(C)	59.	(A)	93.	(D)
26.	(D)	60.	(E)	94.	(B)
27.	(A)	61.	(E)	95.	(E)
28.	(B)	62.	(B)	96.	(A)
29.	(C)	63.	(B)	97.	(E)
30.	(D)	64.	(A)	98.	(C)
31.	(D)	65.	(A)	99.	(B)
32.	(E)	66.	(C)	100.	(C)
33.	(B)	67.	(B)		
34.	(E)	68.	(D)		

PRACTICE TEST 1

Detailed Explanations of Answers

1. **(B)**   The key word in the question is "production." Because production involves the making of the product, choice (B) is correct. Predicting the types of cars different people will buy (A), determining the features of the car (C), selling the car (D), and developing a sales promotion campaign for the car (E) are marketing activities and are therefore not correct answers.

2. **(C)**   Macro-marketing looks at the marketing function in relation to society as a whole, while micro-marketing looks at activities of individual organizations. The dilemma occurs when marketing efforts of individual producers may not be good for society; therefore, (C) is the correct choice. Answers (A), (B), (D), (E), while partially correct statements, do not relate to society as a whole. Thus, they are not examples of the macro-micro dilemma.

3. **(D)**   Marketing information systems help marketing managers with their decision making by making routine information available at the right time. Therefore, this is the correct choice. Decision support systems are computerized systems that help any decision maker, not just marketing managers (A). Time series analysis is a statistical forecasting tool (B), marketing research is helpful for solving non-routine problems (C), and consumer panels are groups of customers who help collect data (E).

4. **(A)**   With an emphasis on selling more parts and outselling the competition, the company is run as if it were in the sales era. (A) is the correct choice. The production era (B) focused on the production of products. The marketing company era (C) is a time when companies embraced the marketing concept. The simple trade era (D) was when middlemen were introduced in the early role of marketing involving simple distribution. The marketing department era (E) tied together various marketing efforts under one department.

5. **(D)**   The "four P's" of a marketing mix are product, price, place, and promotion. These are the controllable variables a company applies in their marketing strategy. (D) is the correct choice. The remaining answers (A), (B), (C), and (E), while they contain portions of the marketing mix and elements important in marketing strategy, are not correct answers.

6. **(B)** Prices in a market-directed economic system vary to allocate resources and distribute income according to consumer preferences, so price is a rough measure of the value of resources used to produce goods and services. (B) is the correct answer. The remaining choices (A), (C), (D), and (E) relate to decisions that may be utilized in some pricing strategies and tactics but do not relate to the role of price at the macro-level of a market-directed economy, and are incorrect choices.

7. **(B)** Marketing applies to both for-profit and nonprofit organizations. Although a nonprofit's primary objective may not be to seek profit, the firm still wants to satisfy customer needs; consequently, the priorities will be different than a for-profit organization. The correct answer is (B). The remaining sentences about marketing are true. Marketing affects products and services that are bought (A) as well as product prices (D). Advertising and sales promotion are areas in the marketing mix (Promotion) (C) and marketing decisions would include how to sell products (E).

8. **(E)** In a pure subsistence economy, family units make all the products they consume; therefore, (E) is correct. In this type of economy, no marketing takes place because marketing doesn't occur unless two or more parties are willing to exchange something for something else, consequently, (A) is incorrect. In a planned economy, the government makes all decisions about the production and distribution of products and services; therefore, (C) is not the correct choice. In a pure subsistence economy, there is no need for middlemen, since marketing does not occur. (D) is not a correct choice.

9. **(A)** Tariffs are taxes on imported products therefore, (A) is the correct choice. Answer (B) describes "price-fixing," an action sometimes taken by companies which is considered illegal in the United States. Quotas are quantities of products that can be moved in or out of a country (C) and is not the correct answer. Extra money paid to officials for favored status is bribery and is illegal in the United States; therefore, (D) is not a correct answer. Tariffs are legal as long as all regulations are followed. (E) is not the correct answer.

10. **(C)** The question relates to a definition. Economies of scale means that as a company produces larger quantities of an item, the cost of producing each item goes down. (C) is the correct answer. Micro-marketing looks at marketing as a set of activities; (A) is incorrect. Possession utility is having the right to use a product; (B) is not correct. The marketing concept looks at satisfying customers needs. (D) is not correct. Transaction efficiency is not an "official" marketing term although it may be used to describe a process, thus, (E) is not correct.

11. **(C)** Along with the FCC guidelines, the Magnuson Act of 1975 ensures that warranties are clear and definite—not deceptive or unfair. The Act states that producers must provide a clearly written warranty; therefore, (C) is the correct choice. U.S. Common Law says (A) producers of goods must warrant their products as merchantable. Although it may reduce the responsibility of the firm (B), that was not the ruling of the Magnuson Act. The UPC code that identifies products with a readable electronic code was developed to speed the handling of fast-selling products (D). The Federal Fair Packaging and Labeling Act of 1966 required goods to be clearly labeled and understandable (E).

12. **(D)** When marketers compare their product to competitors' offerings, they are concerned with the quality and satisfaction of the total product (B, C). A SWOT analysis (A) is a comparison of a company's strengths vs. weaknesses, and opportunities vs. threats, rather than comparing single products. This eliminates (A) and (E) as possible correct answers.

13. **(B)** A deed performed by one party for another at a cost is a service. (B) is the correct choice. (A) Supplies are expense items that do not become a part of a finished product and are tangible. You cannot "hold" a service; therefore, (C) would be an incorrect answer. (A) is not the correct choice. A perishable good (D) is one that is subject to spoil, such as food. Consequently, (D) is not the correct choice. Because the correct answer is (B), choice (E) is not correct.

14. **(C)** Convenience products are products a customer needs but is not willing to shop around for; therefore, (C) is an incorrect choice, because when it comes to convenience products, customers *do not* shop extensively. The three types of convenience products are staples, impulse products, and emergency products. Staples are products that are bought routinely without much thought. Therefore, (A) is a correct statement. If a buyer does not see an impulse product at the right place, the sale will be lost. Therefore, (B) is a true statement, buyer behavior does affect place utility with impulse products. Because they are usually purchased in emergency situations, emergency products are purchased when urgently needed. (D) is a correct statement. (E) is also true. Branding does help customers cut shopping efforts and encourages repeat buying of satisfactory brands.

15. **(B)** In today's modern economy, market competition and product life cycles are changing at a fast pace. The product life cycle shows a firm needs different marketing mixes as a product moves through the cycle. It may no

longer be profitable *just* to sell "me-too" products; firms need to expand their offerings; therefore, (B) is the correct choice. Most of the profits do not go to innovators (A), as profits rarely occur in the product introduction phase. Moreover, the failure rate of new products is high, not low (C), since only 2% of new products make it to market. The FTC ensures that products are safe for public use (D), but does not play a part in the planning of a new product. Since (A), (C), and (D) are incorrect choices, (E) would be eliminated as a correct answer.

16. **(E)** Customers pay for the capital items when they buy it, but for tax purposes the cost is spread over a number of years. Therefore, a long-lasting product that can be depreciated (D) is a capital item. An example of a capital item is an installation, buildings, land rights, or major equipment in any business or company (A); thus, (E) is the correct answer. Office supplies purchased by individuals are not long lasting, nor would a person depreciate office supplies over a number of years; therefore, (B) is not correct. Raw materials (C) are not considered capital items, but instead are expense items.

17. **(D)** All of the symbols are legally registered for the use of a single company. A trademark includes those words, symbols, or marks like (A), (B), and (C). By officially registering their seal, a company is protected legally from those who try to copy the label. Trademarks do not even need to be a word, they can be a symbol (C). (E) is incorrect because all the symbols are trademarks.

18. **(D)** This question relates to different levels of segmentation. Mass marketing (B) is the lowest level that doesn't involve any segmentation at all, and micro-marketing is the highest level of segmentation where firms try to offer products and services to suit individual customers' needs (D). Niche marketing (A) caters to segments within segments of customers. Segment marketing (C) offers different products for different groups of customers (not at the individual level). Macro-marketing deals with marketing at the societal level and is clearly inappropriate in this situation.

19. **(D)** By meeting customers needs better, a better package can help create a "new" product for a "new" market. The packaging of a product (A) does not provide better shelf placement. Consumer demand and extra money paid for shelf space dictate the shelf placement of a product. The average packaging costs are between 1 and 70% rather than over 95% (B). The Federal Packaging and Labeling Act (C) does not hold restrictions on packaging—rather its various laws provide general guidance on packaging issues and the producers can choose whether or not to abide by them. If

consumers do not understand the terminology, labeling can become misleading, but the statement that labels are inaccurate and no one reads them (E) is not true. Many labels are correct and many people do read labels.

20. **(C)** Brand nonrecognition means that final consumers do not recognize a brand at all. (C) is the correct answer. Brand rejection (A) occurs when a customer refuses to buy a certain brand. Brand recognition (B) happens when customers remember the brands they buy. Brand preference (D) means that customers choose one brand over other brands, perhaps out of habit. Brand insistence (E) occurs when customers insist on a firm's branded products and are willing to search for it by any means. Hence, the example in the question clearly demonstrates a customer who is exhibiting brand nonrecognition (C).

21. **(E)** Shopping products the customer sees as basically the same are homogeneous—customers do not think the brand differences are important, they just look at the price. (E) is the correct answer. Specialty products (A) are those that the customer really wants and makes a special effort to find—it does not involve comparing prices or brands. Convenience products (C) are those that a customer needs but is not willing to spend much time shopping for—often bought on an impulse, no comparing is used here either. Regularly sought products (D) is not a division of product class. This term may be confused with regularly unsought products, which are a division of product class.

22. **(A)** Geographical segmentation involves customizing products and services for groups of customers based on where they reside. That is what Progresso Soup seems to be doing in this question. Therefore, the correct answer is (A). Behavioral segmentation (B) is done based on usage behavior. That is not what the question describes. Similarly, demographic (C) and psychographic segmentation (D) can be ruled out since the former deals with users' demographics such as age, occupation, and income while the latter deals with customers' lifestyles. There is no such thing as political segmentation (E), so that can be eliminated.

23. **(A)** is the correct answer because it is the only statement that is entirely not true. Just because industry sales rise doesn't mean that industry profits will also rise. Increased competition among individual companies within the industry could prompt lower selling prices in the industry which would lead to lower profits for the industry. Increased sales could also prompt expensive investments in capital equipment which would decrease profits

if the individual firms are already operating at full capacity. (B) is not the correct answer because the statement is true. Customers' attitudes as well as needs will change over time. Thus, a customer who bought the product in the past may no longer have need for the product, or a customer who previously didn't have a need for the product may acquire a need for the product (target markets may change). (C) is also not correct because the statement is true. Once a product proves its profit potential, everybody will want to sell the product to get a piece of the "profit pie." (D) is also incorrect because the statement is true. Growth refers to sales growth, not necessarily profit growth. Remember, competition enters in this stage, which, in general, tends to decrease profits. (E) is also not correct because although (D) is true, (A) is not true.

24. **(E)** is correct because all of the statements are correct. Industry profits initially do increase (A), but later industry profits start to decline (B). Also, more companies enter the industry because they see that industry profits initially are increasing (C). Furthermore, industry sales increase (D) because of heightened consumer awareness. (A), (B), (C), and (D) are all correct; consequently, (E) is the correct answer.

25. **(C)** Occupation (C) is a demographic segmentation variable and is the correct choice. Social class (A), personality (B), lifestyle (D), and interests (E) are all psychographic segmentation variables.

26. **(D)** The four major categories or bases for segmentation are geographic (A), demographic (B), behavioral (C), and psychographic (E). Therefore, the correct answer is moods (D), which is not one of the four bases noted.

27. **(A)** The demand is elastic. Any increase in price that creates a decrease in total revenue is said to be elastic. (B) is not correct, because in order for the demand to be inelastic, the total revenue would have to have increased. Unitary elasticity (C) occurs when the total revenue stays the same when the price of a product is changed. There is not enough information given to know whether or not the meat is old (D). Elasticity can be determined from the information given, so (E) is incorrect.

28. **(B)** is the correct answer, the demand is elastic. When a firm or organization reduces their price and total revenues increase (or stretch), the demand is said to be elastic. (A) is incorrect. In order for the demand to be unitarily elastic, the revenue would have to stay the same. Inelasticity would occur if the total revenue decreased in conjunction with a decrease in price (C). (D) and (E) are both incorrect. You cannot have elasticity and inelasticity at

the same time, and in the example, revenue of the Yearous Group showed an increase, while the price was dropped.

29. **(C)** is the correct answer. The farmer's crop would most likely be elastic. If the farmer dropped his price, more people would buy his potatoes. Potatoes are a commodity where people shop for the "best buy." (A) is incorrect because the total revenue would, in all likelihood, increase, not decrease, with a price reduction. (B) is incorrect because people shopping for potatoes are price conscious and shop for the least expensive. (D) is incorrect because the total revenue would not stay the same with an increase or decrease in price for this type of product. (E) cannot be true because demand must be elastic, inelastic, or have unitary elasticity.

30. **(D)** Bob would find himself in a situation with unitary elasticity. When raising or lowering the price of your product has no effect on total revenue, the situation is said to have unitary elasticity of demand. (A) is wrong because Bob can make a conclusion about demand. (B) is also incorrect because if the demand were elastic, when the price was dropped, total revenues would increase, and when the price was raised, total revenues would decrease. (C) is also wrong because if it were inelastic, when Bob tried to lower his price, he would find that his total revenue would also be lower, yet if he raised his price, his total revenue would increase. With the information given, we don't know whether he should sell shrimp (E).

31. **(D)** The standard commission used in advertising agencies is 15% of media billing. In this question, 15% of $20,000 is $3,000. Therefore, (D) is the right answer.

32. **(E)** All the answers are examples of retailing. Retailing refers to the selling of products and services to the final consumer. (E) is correct. (A) is a good example of retailing at a college level, with the final consumer being the faculty at the college. (B) is also a type of retailing, although not a pleasant one for the car owner. (C) is door-to-door retailing involving selling a product to a final consumer. (D) is probably the most common type of retailing, where the final consumer goes directly to the point-of-sale for a product.

33. **(B)** The rate of usage, i.e., light, medium, or heavy, is an example of usage behavior and is part of the behavioral segmentation category (B). Geographic segmentation deals with where people reside (A), demographic segmentation is dividing a market based on factors such as age, income, gender, and occupation (C). Psychographic segmentation breaks down a

market based on users' lifestyles (D). Geodemographic segmentation (E) is also incorrect because it is a combination of answers (A) and (C).

34. **(E)** Positioning is giving a product a specific image that differentiates it from its competition (A), and this is done to occupy a certain place in consumers' minds in relation to competing brands (B). Since both (A) and (B) are true statements, the correct answer is (E). Positioning is as important as segmentation, so (C) is incorrect. Also, positioning can be used by any firm regardless of size or status, so (D) too is incorrect.

35. **(B)** is correct because pleasing products are not good for consumers in the long run but do give immediate satisfaction. Disposable diapers satisfy the parents' need for convenience but are not good for the environment and thus are not good for consumers in the long run. (A) is not correct because a desirable product gives immediate satisfaction and is good for consumers in the long run. (C) is not correct because performance products are not a type of new product opportunity. (D) is not correct because deficient products do not satisfy consumers in the long run or provide immediate satisfaction. (E) is not correct because salutary products are good for consumers in the long run but do not give the consumer immediate satisfaction.

36. **(E)** is the correct answer because industry sales do level off in market maturity (A). Profits can increase for a particular company if they have a marketing mix that appeals to consumers (B). (C) is correct because some firms are not efficiently using their product and thus can't compete in the price wars of their more efficient competitors, so they drop out of the industry. Promotion costs rise (D) because firms want to promote their product as different, or they want to remind consumers about the product and its uses to keep sales from falling.

37. **(C)** The American cowboy is a cultural icon used by Stetson in its advertising to reinforce its American roots. Therefore, (C) is the right choice. Stetson's positioning is not based on a particular feature of the product, so (A) is incorrect. It is also not based on Stetson's user profile (B). (D) is incorrect because the question makes no reference to Stetson's competition. Finally, since the question doesn't indicate a tangible product benefit, (E) is incorrect.

38. **(A)** This is a question of evaluating which type of buying method is being used in the process of purchasing a product for this company. The descriptive buying method is a form of buying a product through a written or verbal description and is often done without inspection. This purchase is

usually based on a mutual trust between buyers and sellers and is used to reduce the cost of buying; (A) is the correct choice. There is no such thing as test buying, although it does sound good, so (B) is an invalid answer. Inspection buying is the process of inspecting every item before you buy it; (C) is not the best choice. Sampling buying means looking at only part of the potential purchase, making the assumption that the whole purchase will be of the same standards; (D) is not correct. Negotiated contract buying means agreeing to a contract to purchase, but the contract allows for changes in the purchasing arrangements; (E) is an incorrect choice.

39. **(A)** The Multiple Buying Influence means several people—perhaps even top management—share in making a purchase decision. Because the question pertains to a business, the general public would not influence the decision to purchase a copier. (A) is the correct choice. The next four choices are all part of the Multiple Buying Influence. An influencer (B) could be an engineer or research person who helps to write specifications or supply information for evaluating alternatives. A buyer (C) could be a purchasing agent who has the responsibility for working with suppliers and arranging terms of the sale. Deciders (D) are people in the organization who have the power to select or approve the supplier. A gatekeeper (E) is a person who controls the information throughout the whole organization.

40. **(B)** The business exchange function in a market driven society involves giving an object or service to someone in exchange for money. Money is the price. (A) is incorrect because it is a starting point for price negotiation. Many times wholesalers and retailers are willing to change the "Price" in exchange for quantity purchases, to get rid of out-of-season merchandise, and many other reasons. Price is not calculated by dividing cost by selling price; thus, (C) is incorrect. Cost is how much the product or service "costs," or is paid for, by the intermediary or manufacturer. Adding a markup to that figure gives a price; thus, (D) is not correct. And (E) is not correct because price may be driven by something other than profit, such as sales.

41. **(E)** is the correct choice. The shirt would be marked up $600. To calculate the amount of markup, you use the formula Amount of Markup = Selling Price − Cost. If the shirt sold for $1,000, and the cost to Sally was $400, then $1,000 − $400 = $600. (A), (B), (C), and (D) are incorrect.

42. **(D)** is the correct answer. Percent markup based upon the selling price is calculated by dividing the selling, or retail, price into the amount of the markup. (A) is incorrect because 600/1,000 = 60%, not 10%. Likewise, (B)

and (C) are incorrect. Amount of Markup/Selling Price = Percent Markup, thus the answer can be determined, and (E) is incorrect.

43. **(A)** is the correct choice. If the cost of a product is $400, and the markup percent on the retail selling price is 60%, then, by formula, the selling price is $1,000. The calculation can be made by taking the cost of the product and dividing it by 1 minus the percent of selling price. Thus, (B), (C), (D), and (E) are incorrect. $400/1 − .60 = $1,000.

44. **(C)** is the correct answer. In order to calculate the maximum cost, use the following formula: Cost + Markup = Retail Sales Price.

$$x + (.40)x = 3$$
$$1.4x = 3$$
$$x = 2.14$$

The maximum Ron and Dee can pay per tile is $2.14. Thus, answers (A), (B), and (D) are incorrect. (E) is incorrect because the answer can be determined based on the information provided.

45. **(E)** is the correct answer. If Pake Productions utilizes the new price for the speakers, $160, then their markdown would be 25%. If they utilize the original price as the denominator, then the markdown percentage is 20%. (A) and (B) are both incorrect as they are dollar amounts, not percentages. While 25% (C) is a good answer for calculating the mark-down percentage on the new selling price (Amount of Markdown/New Sales Price, or $40/$ 160), it is not the most correct. Likewise with (D); if Pake calculated the markdown on the original price ($40/$200), this would be the correct answer, although it is not the correct answer for the question. The markdown calculation depends on the accounting system being used. Both markdown methods are common.

46. **(B)** is the correct choice. The terms on an invoice 2/10 net 30, indicate that the buyers will get a two percent discount if they pay the bill early. This is to increase the amount of cash flow for the seller and to encourage early payment of bills. (A) is not the correct choice. If Ogden & Ogden had paid the bill after the ten-day period, this would have been the amount they owed. (C) is also incorrect. However, if Ogden & Ogden had paid the bill after the 30-day net, they may have owed this interest, depending on the payment terms agreed upon between the buyer and seller. (D) and (E) are simply not correct. The Ogden & Ogden Company would not have paid that amount based upon the terms of the invoice.

47. **(B)** Place is the correct answer. By definition, Promotion (A) is communicating information between the seller and potential buyers. Product (C) is the need satisfying offering of a firm. Price (D) is what is charged for something. Consequently, making goods and services available in the right quantities and locations describes Place (B), the correct choice; and (E) is therefore not correct.

48. **(C)** A channel of distribution is any series of firms or individuals who participate in the flow of goods from producer to final user; therefore, (C) is the correct choice. Regrouping activities (A) adjust the quantities and assortments of products handled. Accumulating (B) involves collecting products from many small producers. Bulk-breaking (D) involves dividing larger quantities into smaller quantities. Because (C) is the correct choice, (E) would be incorrect.

49. **(C)** Direct mail (C) is the second-largest category of expense after telemarketing in the direct marketing industry.

50. **(B)** One of the biggest advantages of direct marketing is that firms can tailor their campaign to fit the needs of individual customers (B) Low cost (A) is not necessarily a strong suit of direct marketing, although if done correctly, it is economical only because it is so targeted at specific customers. Both (C) and (D) are incorrect because fast response time cannot be taken for granted (C) and the ability to use J.I.T. is not contingent upon using direct marketing. (E) is incorrect since direct marketing has a low rate of consumer acceptance.

51. **(A)** Selective distribution occurs when a company only sells through middlemen who will give the product special attention; consequently, (A) is the correct answer. Intensive distribution (B) occurs when a company sells a product through all responsible and suitable retailers who will stock and sell the product. Exclusive distribution (C) occurs when a company sells through only one middleman in a particular geographic area. Ideal market exposure (D) makes a product available widely enough to satisfy target customer's needs. Because (A) is the correct choice, (E) cannot be correct.

52. **(C)** A PR "hit" is defined as the number of times a company's name is mentioned in a particular news story (C). PR firms are often evaluated based on the number of "hits" they obtain on behalf of their clients. None of the other choices correctly defines a PR "hit."

53. **(C)** Dual distribution occurs when a producer uses several competing channels to reach the same target market; (C) is the correct answer. Exclusive distribution (A) means that a company sells through only one middleman or one channel. Intensive distribution (B) means selling products through all responsible and suitable sellers. Since (A) and (B) are both incorrect, (D) would not be correct. (E) would also be an incorrect answer because (C) is correct.

54. **(B)** Dual distribution occurs when a producer uses several competing channels to reach the same target market. One reason this occurs is that retailers want large quantities with a lower price per unit; (B) is the best choice. Dual distribution is not needed for convenience products and business suppliers. These types of products are best served by intensive distribution because customers want these products available everywhere. One of the reasons a producer moves toward dual distribution is that current channel members are doing a poor job, so (C) is not a correct answer. (D) is not correct because both (A) and (C) are incorrect and, therefore, (E) cannot be correct either.

55. **(B)** A company newsletter (B) is meant for employees of that firm and is therefore an internal communication device. None of the other choices is truly "internal" since their audiences include "external" stakeholders.

56. **(A)** Horizontal and vertical conflicts are the two basic types of conflicts in channels of distribution. Horizontal conflicts occur between firms at the same level in the channel of distribution. Vertical conflicts occur between firms at different levels of the channel of distribution. (A) is the correct answer. Discrepancy of quantity (B) means the difference between the quantity of products it is economical for a producer to make and the quantity final users or consumers want. Discrepancy of assortment means the difference between the lines a typical producer makes and the assortment final consumers or users want. Assorting (C) means putting together a variety of products, and sorting means separating products into grades. (D) is not a correct choice because both (B) and (C) are incorrect, and (E) is not correct because (A) is the correct answer.

57. **(B)** is the correct choice. Services included are on-time delivery, quality control, custom design, nationwide distribution systems, along with technical advice. (A) is incorrect because prices are often elastic, requiring the firm to price at or near the prices of their competitors. This keeps prices stable. (C) is also incorrect. Industrial marketing is unique for environmen-

tal services, but is not the *most* emphasized area. The distribution emphasis is just to make sure products are available, so (D) is not the correct answer. And even though there is an element of sales promotion in an industrial setting, this is not the most emphasized element of the industrial mix; thus, (E) is incorrect.

58. **(C)**   The example shows administered pricing, so (C) is the correct choice. In administered pricing, the seller sets the price and the buyer pays that listed price. If a price is determined through the use of sealed or open bids, it is called bid pricing. Thus, (A) is incorrect. In negotiated pricing, there is a stated list price; however, discounting is used to entice purchases. (B) is therefore incorrect. This is not a retail situation, so retail pricing is an incorrect answer (D). In economic pricing (E), the business environment has more of an impact on the price set than the seller, so this is a wrong choice.

59. **(A)**   A perceptual map is a two-dimensional diagram that depicts a brand's "position" along two product attributes in relation to its competition. Therefore, (A) is the correct answer. The perceptual map has very little to do with either product design (B) or packaging (C). (D) and (E) imply geographical maps and thus are incorrect.

60. **(E)**   Advertising can make customers aware of all of these areas; thus, (E) is the correct answer. Advertisements allow customers to become aware of new products or brands that they may not otherwise be aware of (A). Additionally, advertising allows the customer to become exposed to product features (B). Advertising can expose potential customers to organizations (C) and customer representatives (D). In summary, advertising is used to reach customers for all of the reasons listed in the answers.

61. **(E)**   All of the statements are true; therefore, (E) is the correct answer. Marketing strategy can help develop flexibility in providing additional customer service, so (A) is incorrect. Marketing strategy provides a road map, giving the marketers a direction and showing what types of expertise are needed, thus facilitating the hiring of high-quality personnel (B), so this answer is not correct. Effective strategy planning is proactive in giving solutions to potential problems, thus (C) is also not true. An effective marketing strategy plan can provide for the utilization of high technology to decrease overall service costs to customers, so (D) is also not true.

62. **(B)**   Marketing activities undertaken by groups without an objective of profit, ROI, or market share are called nonbusiness marketing activities.

An example of such an activity may be a beer manufacturer running an ad campaign to reduce teenage drinking. (A) is incorrect because they are not, or should not, be a waste of time. They may be providing useful information to the listener or viewer. (C) is incorrect; although they may be strategic in nature, the purpose is nonbusiness. Promotional marketing activities (D) refer to activities and processes undertaken as a part of the promotional mix (i.e., advertising, public relations, sales promotion, selling) and is incorrect. Nonmarketing activities (E) is incorrect, because these are marketing functions and activities.

63. **(B)** Salespersons are classified as being order getters, order takers, or missionaries. A department store salesperson who performs a cashier's role is essentially involved in taking orders (B) from customers. The salesperson is not actively soliciting orders (A) nor is that person helping other sales personnel complete an order (D). A PR specialist is far removed from any sales-oriented task, so (C) is incorrect. A copywriter is one who writes copy for advertisements, so (E) too is incorrect.

64. **(A)** TQM (Total Quality Management) describes how companies can use quality to create value and enhance customer satisfaction. This is the perfect choice for the question since it applies in all situations (A). Low prices (B), manufacturing superiority (C), celebrity advertising (D), and sales promotions (E) represent just part of the solution toward creating value and customer satisfaction. They are not sufficient by themselves. Therefore, they are incorrect answers.

65. **(A)** Although many people think money is very important, it is not a level in the hierarchy of needs. (A) is the correct choice. Safety needs (B) are concerns about personal protection and well-being and are a level in the hierarchy of needs. Physiological needs (C) are needs for food, drink, rest, and sex and are a level in the hierarchy of needs. Social needs (D) are needs for love, friendship, status, esteem, and acceptance by others and are also a level in the hierarchy of needs. Since (A) is the answer, (E) would be an incorrect choice.

66. **(C)** The definition of learning is a change in a person's thought processes caused by prior experience; therefore, (C) is the correct answer. A cue (A) is a product sign, ad, or other stimuli in the environment. Responses (B) are efforts to satisfy a strong stimulus that encourages action. A belief (D) is a person's opinion about something. Reinforcement (E) occurs when a response is followed by satisfaction. Cue, response, belief, and reinforcement all occur during the learning process.

67. **(B)** In psychographics or lifestyle analysis, marketers use AIO to analyze people's day-to-day patterns of behavior. A stands for Activities, I stands for Interests, and O stands for opinions, making (B) the correct choice. Any other combinations as in (A), (C), (D), and (E) would be incorrect choices.

68. **(D)** The current trend in business is target marketing whereby marketers have to clearly define their target market and then try to customize an offer for them. The mass-marketing model no longer holds good given the tremendous diversity of customer needs. Therefore, (D) is the right answer. Target marketing (A), segmentation (B), and positioning (C) are all geared toward the current trend in marketing management. Direct marketing (E) is growing and is therefore incorrect.

69. **(E)** Positioning is defined as the process of creating a favorable image of your brand in relation to competing brands. Therefore, (E) is the correct answer. Mass marketing (A) is marketing to everyone with a standardized offering, not just target customers. Target marketing (B) and segmentation (C) deal with breaking up a heterogeneous market into smaller and distinct homogeneous submarkets. Green marketing (D) is environmentally friendly marketing.

70. **(B)** Extensive problem-solving occurs for a completely new or important need involving high involvement in how to satisfy it. The best answer is a washing machine (B) because there is typically high involvement in such a major purchase. Milk (A) and toilet paper (D) purchases are routinized behaviors requiring little involvement. Buying a pair of shoes (C) and T-shirts (E) involve limited problem-solving.

71. **(E)** The adoption process comprises the steps people go through on the journey toward accepting or rejecting a new idea. Payment (E) is not one of these steps. The six steps are as follows: Awareness (C), Interest, Evaluation, Trial (B), Decision (D), and Confirmation (A).

72. **(D)** New product development deals with developing ideas for new products and is not a function of channels of distribution; therefore, (D) is the correct answer. Alleviating discrepancies in assortment (A) and in quantity (B) are both function of distribution channels. Because providing customer service is integrated in all aspects of marketing, (C) is also a function. Creating channels of distribution create time, place, and possession utility, so (E) is also a function of distribution.

73. **(C)** Transforming is not used as a regrouping activity by channel specialists; therefore, (C) is the correct choice. Regrouping activities adjust

the quantities and assortments of products handled. Assorting (A) means putting together a variety of products. Accumulating (B) involves collecting products from many small producers. Bulk-breaking (D) involves dividing larger quantities into smaller quantities. Sorting (E) means separating products into grades and qualities desired by the target market.

74. **(D)** In a complex selling situation that calls for high levels of persuasion, personal selling is often thought to be more effective than advertising primarily because of the direct interaction between the buyer and seller. Thus, (D) is the right answer. Personal selling is one of the most expensive methods of promotion on a per contact basis, so (A) is incorrect. In a given time period, advertising can reach a lot more people than personal selling. Thus, (B) is incorrect. Personal selling is much more effective when the demand is elastic because that is when the demand changes substantially in response to changes in price. So, (C) is incorrect. (E) is also incorrect since (A) and (B) are false.

75. **(E)** Vertical channel integration is the combining of two or more stages of the channel under one management. (E) is the best answer. A strategic alliance (A) is a partnership formed to create a competitive advantage on a worldwide bases. Horizontal channel integration (B) deals with combining institutions at the same level of operation. Reverse channels (C) are used to retrieve products that consumers no longer want. An oligopoly (D) is a competitive structure existing when a few sellers control the supply of a large proportion of a product.

76. **(A)** The best type of distribution for this scenario would be intensive distribution, because sellers want the product to be easily reached by everyone. Exclusive distribution (B) is using a single outlet and would not answer the request for availability. Vertical distribution (C) and horizontal distribution (D) are not types of distribution. Selective distribution (E) means using only some available outlets to distribute a product, which also would not satisfy the availability factor.

77. **(D)** The definition of exclusive distribution is using a single outlet in a fairly large geographic area to distribute a product or service; therefore, (D) is the correct answer. Exclusive distribution also creates the "mystique" marketers want to make the product more appealing. Selective distribution (A) is used when you want middlemen to give a product special attention. Selective distribution uses many outlets to distribute the product but not as many as intensive. Universal distribution (B) would not be correct because

it is not a distribution classification. Intensive distribution (C) would not be correct because sellers do want the product to be easily reached by everyone. In exclusive distribution, sellers only want the product to be available to those who can afford the product.

78. **(C)** E-commerce has been plagued by concerns about security and identity theft (C). Although advances in encryption technology have alleviated some of these fears, it is still the biggest deterrent to sales among the choices outlined in this question. None of the other choices correctly identifies a major concern of e-commerce.

79. **(C)** Exclusive dealing forbids an intermediary to carry products of a competing manufacturer. A tying agreement (A) requires a channel member to buy other products from a supplier besides the one preferred by the channel member. A monopoly (B) involves a market structure that exists when an organization produces a product that has no close substitutes and becomes the sole source of supply. A strategic channel alliance (D) is a marketing channel that exists when the products of one organization are distributed through the marketing channels of another organization. A vertical marketing system (E) occurs when channel activities are coordinated by a single channel member to achieve efficient, low-cost distribution aimed at satisfying the target market.

80. **(A)** A coupon for a bag of chips on a bottle of Pepsi is an example of a cross-promotion that is specifically referred to as a "cross-ruff coupon" (A). In this case, Pepsi could have a tie-in agreement with its own Frito-Lay business unit, which is marketing the potato chips so the corporation benefits from the cross-promotion. Cross-ruff promotions are also done with other companies. None of the other terms correctly describes this promotional offer by Pepsi.

81. **(C)** Most contemporary brands are positioned in consumers' minds with respect to their features. For instance, Dell tries to position its computer as being "easy-to-use." Therefore, (C) is the best choice. Although all the other options, which includes against a competitor (A), away from a competitor (B), user's lifestyle (D), and user's occupation (E), are valid positioning characteristics, they are relatively less popular compared to product attributes.

82. **(E)** The three "pillars" of the marketing concept are customer satisfaction, team effort, and the firm's objective. In this question, only customer satisfaction (E) appears as one of the choices. None of the other choices are in the marketing concept and, therefore, are incorrect.

83. **(B)** When a company chooses one attribute to excel at and promotes it to create a competitive advantage, it is called a unique selling proposition. Thus, (B) is the right answer. There is no such thing as overpositioning (A). Undifferentiated marketing (C) is when a company chooses to mass market its product or service. Relationship marketing (D) is when companies aim to create lasting relationships with its stakeholders. Concentrated marketing (E) is also incorrect because it is a segmentation strategy where companies target one segment to pursue with a unique marketing mix.

84. **(B)** E-commerce and other Internet-based firms prefer flexible and dynamic pricing policies (B) compared to the other choices that are more restrictive in nature.

85. **(A)** This question deals with brand sponsor decisions. Manufacturers' brands, such as Heinz ketchup, dominate the American scene. Many manufacturers create their own brand and some even rent well-known brand names by paying royalties. Choices (B), (C), and (D) are all private brands owned by Sears. Sears (a retailer) does not produce many of the products that carry its name, but instead contracts with manufacturers to produce these products on the chain's behalf. Thus, these are incorrect choices. Because (A) is the best answer, (E) cannot be correct.

86. **(C)** This question deals with the broad topic of brand decisions. A company may be able to use any one of these decisions for its products. The strategy described in this question relates to the multibrand decision, so (C) is the correct answer. Brand repositioning (A) may be needed if a competitor launched a brand that competes directly with an existing product. Brand extension decisions (B) relate to any effort to use a successful brand name to launch product modifications or new products. Family brands (D) are created by manufacturers who brand their products. Brand quality (E) supports the brand decision in the target market.

87. **(C)** Setting low prices is consistent with penetration pricing and current profit maximization. Therefore, (C) is the logical answer. Low prices do not always translate into higher market share. Thus, (A) is incorrect. Similarly, low prices do not guarantee superior product quality (B) or survival in the market (D). Just-in-time is an inventory management tool that has very little to do with low prices; thus, (E) is also incorrect.

88. **(C)** The basic difference between fixed and variable costs is that fixed costs do not change with the volume of output, while variable costs do. Rent, heating bills, air-conditioning costs, interest payments, and executive

salaries are all expenses that do not change with the level of output. So, they are fixed costs and the correct answer is (C). There is no such thing as monopoly costs (E) or independent costs (D). They are also not standard costs (A) or variable costs (B).

89. **(C)** This question pertains to a company's product line-stretching decisions. Line stretching occurs when a company lengthens its product line beyond its current range. A company may stretch downward for any of the above reasons except (C). Therefore, (C) is the correct answer. When a company decides to stretch upward, it may be because the company at the lower end of the market may want to enter the higher end (C).

90. **(A)** Globalization has resulted in a big surge in competition both in the U.S. market and overseas. Because of increasing competition, more and more companies are consolidating their promotion activities in the form of Integrated Marketing Communications. Therefore, (A) is the correct choice. Advertising costs are on the rise, so (B) is untrue. There is no evidence that sales promotion is on the decline (C) or that costs of personal selling have gone up across the board (D). Since IMC may use many different kinds of media, (E) is incorrect.

91. **(B)** This is a definitional question since only single-source data systems allow managers to link TV advertising to store choice behavior (B). Motivational research is a type of qualitative marketing research that seeks in-depth answers from respondents (A). The Peoplemeter is used by A.C. Nielsen to measure TV ratings (C). Subliminal research is also irrelevant here since it involves subliminal perception (D). Focus groups are also a qualitative research method (E).

92. **(A)** is the right choice because the industrial structure shapes a country's product and service needs, income, and employment levels. The income distribution determines if the income of the population in that country would create a market for the product. These things are economically important. Political stability and attitudes (B) and cultural environment and government bureaucracy (C) are not really economic factors that reflect the country's attractiveness. Rather, they are factors that are involved in the political-legal attractiveness of the country environmentally. (D) and (E) do not deal with why one does business in a foreign country; they are actually dealing with *how* one does business.

93. **(D)** is correct. An industrializing economy needs more imports of certain products as manufacturing increases. A subsistence economy (A) offers

few market opportunities and a rich class seldom exists. A raw-material-exporting economy (B) gains much of their revenues from exporting one particular natural resource; therefore, their economy has either a poor class or wealthy upper class. An industrialized economy (C) has varied manufacturing activities and a large middle class. Answer (E) is incorrect because one of the above is indeed true.

94. **(B)**   Marketers could either try to actively manage the environment (proactive) or merely react to changes later (reactive). Successful companies always choose the former rather than the latter. Therefore, (B) is the best choice. None of the other choices can be generalized to *all* successful companies.

95. **(E)**   Exporting is the simplest way to enter a foreign market because all of the goods are manufactured or produced in the home country. In joint venturing (A), the company has to join with a partner to set up production facilities abroad which help to complicate entry, and dilute control. Licensing (B) and management contracting (C) are methods, or types, of joint venturing and are not correct. Direct investment (D) has the biggest involvement because the company develops foreign-based assembly or manufacturing facilities. This makes the entry into the foreign market much more difficult, not simple.

96. **(A)**   is correct. Straight extension is the only strategy for marketing a product in a foreign market without any product changes. Product adaptation (B) by definition involves changing the product to meet the local conditions. Certain aspects of the product such as packaging, branding, or labeling can be changed. Product invention (C) consists of creating something new. Both communication adaptation (D) and dual adaptation (E) are promotional strategies, not product strategies, and are incorrect choices.

97. **(E)**   Direct investment involves the highest risk (E). Direct investment risks include devalued currencies, falling markets, and government takeover (nationalization). Exporting (A) involves very little risk because the company can passively export surpluses from time to time, or it can actively commit to the country. While joint venturing (B) often gives a company less control, it doesn't involve as much risk as direct investment. Joint ownership (C) is a type of joint venturing, and is incorrect. Licensing (D) is also a type of joint venturing, so it is incorrect.

98. **(C)**   Management contracting is the best answer because the domestic firm is exporting services rather than products. With licensing (A), the

company may give up not only potential profits, but it could also create a competitor when the contract ends. Contract manufacturing (B) provides less control over the manufacturing process and a loss of potential profits. Joint ownership (D) provides the risk that the partners could disagree over issues such as investment and marketing strategies. (E) is incorrect since both (A) and (B) are not correct answers.

99. **(B)** Before the 1980s, regulation of the country's transportation systems was intense. The federal government set the rates that could be charged by the carriers. Therefore, carriers could not compete on price as they do now. The carriers had to compete with the other variables of the marketing mix, and often had increases in promotion (A). The government did not tell the carriers where to ship (C), so that is incorrect. Product offerings (D) and service offerings (E) are also incorrect because the carriers were competing in these areas to make up for the lack of differences in cost.

100. **(C)** Rebates are a common form of sales promotion similar to coupons, sweepstakes, and special sales offers that offer temporary incentives to customers to try a product. Therefore, (C) is the right answer. Advertising is a form of mass communication aimed at a large audience, so (A) is incorrect. Direct marketing involves a direct communication between the buyer and seller usually involving an immediate response, so (B) is incorrect. Personal selling involves a direct face-to-face interaction between the buyer and seller, so (D) is incorrect. Public relations (E) is also incorrect since rebate offers do not constitute publicity for a firm.

PRACTICE TEST 2

CLEP Principles of Marketing

Also available at the REA Study Center (*www.rea.com/studycenter*)

This practice test is also offered online at the REA Study Center. Since all CLEP exams are administered on computer, we recommend that you take the online version of this test to simulate test-day conditions and to receive these added benefits:

- **Timed testing conditions** – helps you gauge how much time you can spend on each question
- **Automatic scoring** – find out how you did on the test, instantly
- **On-screen detailed explanations of answers** – gives you the correct answer and explains why the other answer choices are wrong
- **Diagnostic score reports** – pinpoint where you're strongest and where you need to focus your study

PRACTICE TEST 2

CLEP Principles of Marketing

(Answer sheets appear in the back of the book.)

TIME: 90 Minutes
100 Questions

DIRECTIONS: Each of the questions or incomplete statements below is followed by five possible answers or completions. Select the best choice in each case and fill in the corresponding oval on the answer sheet.

1. Based upon retail selling price, if John Doe wants to figure out the actual amount of markup of a product he plans to retail, he should

   (A) divide the selling price by the cost
   (B) divide the cost by the selling price
   (C) subtract the cost from the selling price
   (D) subtract the cost from the markup
   (E) Cannot be determined from the information given

2. With a selling price of $2,000 and a cost of $800, what would the markup (at retail) be for this product?

   (A) $1,000
   (B) $2,000
   (C) $1,200
   (D) $800
   (E) $1,250

3. Joe Fisherman wants to know his percent markup on retail of a pair of shoes for which he paid $1,000. He knows the amount of markup was $600. Which of the following would answer his question?

   (A) 40%
   (B) 150%
   (C) 50%
   (D) 60%
   (E) 100%

400 x .6

4. The MOLE, a toy retailer, wants to calculate the selling price for some of their stuffed dolls. They know that they paid $400 each for the dolls, and they want a 60% markup on selling price. What should their selling price be?

(A) $640
(B) $350
(C) $750
(D) $1,000
(E) $5,300

*400
x .6
240.0*

5. Jan and Bob Winfield want to calculate the cost of a new chair they just bought. Jan told Bob that the retail selling price of the chair was $1,000, and that the markup percent on the selling price was 60%. What would their cost be?

(A) $1,000
(B) $600
(C) $625
(D) $400
(E) $150

1000 x .6

$$\frac{1000 - .6}{1000}$$

6. The McHenry Store, a retailer of fine clothing, wants to calculate both the cost and selling price of a new suit they received from a fine clothing tailor. The amount of markup on selling price is 20%, and the amount of markup is $100. Can they calculate both the cost and the selling price of the product?

(A) Definitely not; they must have more information.
(B) Certainly; the selling price is $500 and the cost is $400.
(C) Certainly; the selling price is $1,000 and the cost is $400.
(D) Of course they can; the selling price is $500 and the cost is $200.
(E) Yes; the cost is $100 and the selling price is $120.

7. When trying to calculate markup based on product cost, Doc and Den wanted to determine the markup on a product that cost $150 and sold for $200. What is their markup?

(A) $25
(B) $40
(C) $50
(D) $60
(E) $110

8. Which of the following is a marketing management tool that shows how customers perceive proposed and/or present brands?

   (A) Market segmentation
   (B) Diversification
   (C) Market penetration
   (D) Brand equity
   (E) Positioning

9. Judy and Dale want to calculate the selling price (on COST) of an item that has a cost of $10.00 and a markup percent on cost of 40%. What is their selling price?

   (A) $16.67
   (B) $10.00
   (C) $10.50
   (D) $12.00
   (E) $14.00

10. Which of the following statements about positioning is FALSE? Positioning techniques

   (A) require a firm to collect data about consumer perceptions of products
   (B) are sometimes called perceptual mapping techniques
   (C) typically rely on a "product space" diagram to show the relationship among competing products
   (D) may use information on consumers' "ideal products" so that the preferences of different consumer segments can be considered
   (E) place products on a graph based on price level and quantity demanded

11. When entering a foreign market, a marketer may need to adapt or modify which of the following promotional methods to meet the culture norms of the target market?

   (A) Theme
   (B) Copy color
   (C) Product's name
   (D) Media
   (E) All of the above

12. When preparing to market internationally, what is the typical chronological progression (or order) that most companies would follow?

   (A) Export department; international division; multinational organization
   (B) International division; export department; multinational organization
   (C) Multinational organization; international division; export department
   (D) Multinational organization; export department; international division
   (E) Export department; multinational organization; international division

13. Sugar Bear Fresh Farm Produce is a premium item sold in exclusive stores where freshness and quality are crucial. Which form of transportation should Sugar Bear Fresh Farm Produce utilize in order to get their goods from Colorado to Pennsylvania?

   (A) They shouldn't ship that far.
   (B) Air
   (C) Water
   (D) Train
   (E) Pipeline

14. When a demand curve is "inelastic,"

   (A) total revenues go down if price goes down
   (B) total revenues go down if price goes up
   (C) total revenues stay the same if price goes down
   (D) total revenues stay the same if price goes up
   (E) total revenues go up if price goes down

15. Which of the following is the best choice when large volumes of goods must be stored regularly?

   (A) Private warehouse
   (B) Public warehouse
   (C) Distribution center
   (D) Containerization
   (E) All of the above should be utilized to store goods regularly.

16. All of the following are criticisms leveled against marketing by critics EXCEPT

(A) selling shoddy or unsafe products
(B) forcing consumers to shop online
(C) using high pressure selling
(D) using deceptive advertising
(E) having excessive markups

17. You finally decided (after some coaxing from your friends) that a good way to get into shape is in-line skating. You **suddenly** become aware of television and radio advertising about Rollerblade products. This is an example of

(A) selective retention
(B) selective perception
(C) selective response
(D) selective exposure
(E) None of the above

18. Advertising belongs to which aspect of the marketing mix?

(A) Product
(B) Price
(C) Place
(D) Promotion
(E) Perception

19. The way a product is perceived by customers on important attributes is called

(A) product position
(B) image psychology
(C) market segmentation
(D) BCG matrix
(E) product life cycle

20. Choosing a product difference that competitors cannot easily copy would be an example of which of the following kinds of differentiation?

    (A) Important
    (B) Distinctive
    (C) Superior
    (D) Preemptive
    (E) Vertical

21. Which of the following types of advertising develops primary demand for a product category as opposed to demand for a specific brand?

    (A) Institutional
    (B) Competitive
    (C) Product
    (D) Reminder
    (E) Pioneering

22. Burdwick's Menswear Store has decided to segment its market based on gender, income, and occupation. Which of the following would most appropriately describe their form of segmentation?

    (A) Geographic segmentation
    (B) Demographic segmentation
    (C) Benefit segmentation
    (D) Psychographic segmentation
    (E) Behavioral segmentation

23. When a company enters a new product category for which its current brand names are not appropriate, it will likely follow which strategy?

    (A) Product extension
    (B) Line extension
    (C) Brand extension
    (D) New brand
    (E) Variety seeking

24. Which of the following dimensions of service marketing refers to the notion that the quality of a service depends upon who provides it as well as when, where, and how it is provided?

    (A) Intangibility
    (B) Inseparability
    (C) Perishability
    (D) Homogeneity
    (E) Variability

25. When choosing the best medium to deliver a firm's message, the first and most important factor to be decided is

    (A) the package design of the product
    (B) to specify the target market and target audience
    (C) to choose the most expensive medium because the most money spent will guarantee the greatest effectiveness
    (D) the products' placement in a store
    (E) the medium the competitive producers are using

26. The stage of the product life cycle characterized by overcapacity, intense competition, and the eventual elimination of weaker competitors is called the

    (A) maturity stage
    (B) introduction stage
    (C) growth stage
    (D) decline stage
    (E) renewal stage

27. If Mark pays the Hershey Company for the right to use its name on his line of T-shirts, then Mark is using which strategy?

    (A) Manufacturer's branding
    (B) Licensed branding
    (C) Co-branding
    (D) Private branding
    (E) Line extension

28. Which type of new product test is most likely to answer the questions: "How does the customer perceive the product?" and "Who would use the product?"

    (A) An internal test
    (B) A concept test
    (C) Commercialization
    (D) Weighted point system
    (E) Non-weighted point system

29. The process of offering a product for sale on a limited basis in a defined geographic area in order to gauge consumer reaction to the actual product is known as

    (A) selected controlled markets
    (B) store audits
    (C) standard markets
    (D) test markets
    (E) None of the above

30. What is meant by commercialization of a new product?

    (A) Create a product prototype.
    (B) Test the product and product strategy in the marketplace.
    (C) Position and offer the product in the marketplace.
    (D) Identify the new product niche.
    (E) None of the above.

31. Which of the following are NOT examples of support goods?

    (A) Services
    (B) Supplies
    (C) Installations
    (D) Accessory equipment
    (E) All of the above are examples of support goods

32. The manufacturing of a telephone, using various raw materials, is an example of what type of utility?

    (A) Task
    (B) Possession
    (C) Time
    (D) Form
    (E) Place

33. In macro-marketing, which of the following universal functions of marketing have to be performed?

    (A) Buying
    (B) Transporting
    (C) Marketing information
    (D) All of the above
    (E) None of the above

34. The marketing concept came to the forefront of American business during which of the following eras?

    (A) Simple trade era
    (B) Marketing department era
    (C) Production era
    (D) Sales era
    (E) Marketing company era

35. Which of the following is NOT a step in the approach to segmenting *product markets*?

    (A) Name the possible product markets.
    (B) List the potential customer needs.
    (C) Estimate the size of the product market segments.
    (D) Form a heterogeneous market.
    (E) All of the above are steps in the process.

36. Which of the following is the best example of product development?

    (A) American Express increased advertising expenditures to encourage customers to use the card when they went out to dinner, not just for shopping.
    (B) To reach new customers, Taco Bell opened new retail outlets in airports, office buildings, zoos, and hospitals.
    (C) Suave boosted sales by introducing a new line of shampoo products.
    (D) Nintendo purchased Cover Girl and expanded into cosmetic products.
    (E) None of the above are good examples of product development.

37. A routine repurchase that may have been made many times before is called

    (A) new-task buying
    (B) straight rebuy
    (C) modified rebuy
    (D) purchase
    (E) None of the above

38. Employers hire buying specialists. These specialists are called what?

    (A) Purchasing agents
    (B) Sales managers
    (C) Order takers
    (D) Order getters
    (E) Any of the above

39. By evaluating suppliers and how they are working out for a company, buyers can make better (and more informed) decisions. A formal rating of suppliers on all relevant areas of performance is called a(n)

    (A) evaluation
    (B) check-list
    (C) vendor analysis
    (D) subjective interpretation
    (E) buyer analysis

40. Multiple buying influence means that several people share in making purchase decisions. These people are called

    (A) users
    (B) buyers
    (C) influencers
    (D) gatekeepers
    (E) All of the above

41. What type of buying is required for nonstandardized products that require careful examination?

    (A) Negotiated contract buying
    (B) Inspection buying
    (C) Sampling buying
    (D) Description buying
    (E) Routinized response buying

42. Which of the following is the first step in undertaking a marketing research project?

(A) Define the problem.
(B) Solve the problem.
(C) Collect problem-specific data.
(D) Analyze the situation.
(E) Define a sample.

43. Which of the following steps of the market research process typically takes over half of the time in completing the research?

(A) Problem definition
(B) Situational analysis
(C) Data collection
(D) Problem-solving
(E) Alternative development

44. A research proposal

(A) is stated right after the problem is defined
(B) is a plan that specifies what information will be obtained and how
(C) can include information about costs
(D) Only (A) and (C) are correct
(E) Only (B) and (C) are correct

45. Which of the following research methods require the most care in interpreting the results?

(A) Random sampling
(B) Mail surveys
(C) Telephone surveys
(D) Personal interview surveys
(E) All of the above

46. Marketing research

(A) should be planned by research specialists who understand research techniques better than marketing managers
(B) consists mainly of survey design and statistical techniques
(C) is only needed by producers who have long channels of distribution
(D) is needed to keep isolated marketing managers in touch with their markets
(E) should not be an ongoing process

47. Which of the following is a major *disadvantage* associated with the collection of primary data in the course of marketing research?

    (A) It provides the most recent data possible.
    (B) It is typically expensive.
    (C) It allows for secrecy from competitors.
    (D) It fits the firm's marketing needs well.
    (E) Data collection is rapid.

48. The birthrate in the United States is currently

    (A) starting to drop because more couples are waiting to have children
    (B) rising sharply due to returning soldiers starting new families
    (C) rising sharply due to the abundance of women at the child-bearing age
    (D) dropping because more women are entering the workforce and there is less of a want for large families
    (E) Both (A) and (D) are correct.

49. The United States

    (A) and England have the highest divorce rate in the world—about 45% of marriages end in divorce
    (B) has the lowest divorce rate in the world—about 12% of marriages end in divorce
    (C) has the highest divorce rate in the world—about 38% of marriages end in divorce
    (D) and England have the lowest divorce rate in the world—about 24% of marriages end in divorce
    (E) has a divorce rate of about 13%

50. A widely available measure of the output of the whole economy and the total market value of goods and services produced in a year in the United States is called

    (A) economic systems
    (B) gross domestic product
    (C) gross sales
    (D) gross margin
    (E) gross national product

51. The income that is left after taxes for a family to make payments on necessities is called

    (A) gross profit
    (B) disposable income
    (C) net profit
    (D) discretionary income
    (E) family income

52. Sales promotion refers to promotion activities that stimulate interest, trial, or purchase by consumers. It would thus include activities other than

    (A) advertising
    (B) publicity
    (C) personal selling
    (D) point-of-purchase materials
    (E) (A), (B), and (C) are correct

53. With regard to Internet marketing, which of the following statements is FALSE?

    (A) Use of e-mail is growing.
    (B) Business-to-business advertising is growing on the Internet.
    (C) Primary users of the Internet are baby boomers.
    (D) Primary users of the Internet are college students and Generation X.
    (E) It allows sellers to learn more about buyers.

54. Managers who are satisfied with their current market share and profit situation sometimes adopt "status quo" objectives. Which of the following phrases would not be used in status quo pricing?

    (A) Meet competition.
    (B) Stabilize prices.
    (C) Avoid competition.
    (D) Slightly raise prices.
    (E) Promote more aggressively.

55. During the communication process, the same message may be interpreted differently by the various audiences. How the message is translated by the buyer/receiver is called

    (A) decoding
    (B) encoding
    (C) noise
    (D) source
    (E) receiver

56. The adoption curve, which shows how products are adopted once introduced into the market place, defines several different groups, and how they accept ideas. The largest percentage of adopters fall into which group(s)?

    (A) Innovators
    (B) Early adopters
    (C) Early and late majority
    (D) Late majority
    (E) Laggards or nonadopters

57. "Pulling" a product through the distribution channel refers to

    (A) using normal promotional efforts in order to help sell the whole marketing mix to possible channel members
    (B) getting customers to ask intermediaries (or middlemen) for the product
    (C) promotion to employees
    (D) using only one promotion "blend" for all situations
    (E) using highly expensive and aggressive promotions

58. Selective demand for a company's own brand would most likely occur in which stage of the product life cycle?

    (A) Market introduction
    (B) Market growth
    (C) Market maturity
    (D) Sales decline
    (E) Competition decline

59. An example of a sales promotion activity aimed at a final consumer or user could be

    (A) banners and streamers
    (B) promotional allowances
    (C) sales contests
    (D) bonuses
    (E) training materials

60. Trucks are expensive, but much more flexible than other types of transportation modes. Approximately what percentage of consumer products travel from the producer to the final consumer by truck?

    (A) 25%
    (B) 50%
    (C) 33%
    (D) 66%
    (E) 75%

61. If a firm's total revenue decreases when the price of its product is raised from $50 to $55, the demand for this product between these two prices is

    (A) unitary elastic
    (B) elastic
    (C) inelastic
    (D) static
    (E) Cannot tell from the information given

62. Pure competition occurs when a market has

    (A) many buyers and sellers
    (B) informed buyers and sellers
    (C) homogeneous (similar) products
    (D) easy entry for new sellers
    (E) All of the above are true

63. The firm can vary its marketing mix through the storing function of physical distribution in which of the following ways?

    (A) Adjusting the time the goods are held
    (B) Sharing the storing costs
    (C) Delegating the job to a specialized storing facility
    (D) All of the above
    (E) None of the above

64. Storing is the marketing function of holding goods. Which of the following economic utilities does it provide?

    (A) Time
    (B) Place
    (C) Possession
    (D) Ownership
    (E) All of the above

65. The *Wall Street Journal* has been trying to attract new customers by promoting its newspaper for student use in business classes. This is an example of

    (A) product development
    (B) diversification
    (C) market penetration
    (D) market development
    (E) target marketing

66. When groups of shippers pool their shipments together, what is this called?

    (A) Containerization
    (B) Piggyback service
    (C) Pool car service
    (D) Diversion in transit
    (E) Birdyback service

67. A tariff is a

    (A) limit on the amount of goods the importing country will accept
    (B) tax levied by a government against imported products
    (C) total ban on imports
    (D) method of entering a foreign market through a licensing arrangement
    (E) boycott of imports by the steel industry of the U.S.

68. In relation to Maslow's hierarchy of needs, the need for self-esteem, accomplishment, fun, freedom, and relaxation are attributed to which of the following needs?

   (A) Physiological
   (B) Safety
   (C) Self-actualization
   (D) Love and belongingness
   (E) Esteem, love and belongingness

69. Differences in perceptions affect how consumers gather and inter pret infor- mation from their environment. The selective processes influencing these perceptions include

   (A) selective retention
   (B) selective perception
   (C) selective exposure
   (D) selective response
   (E) Only (A), (B), and (C) are correct

70. Countertrade is

   (A) illegal in the U.S.
   (B) found only in planned economies
   (C) a transaction that may not involve an exchange of money
   (D) found only in subsistence economies
   (E) Both (B) and (D) are true

71. "Psychographics" is (are)

   (A) lifestyle analyses
   (B) the study of "who wears the pants in the household" in terms of purchases
   (C) an analysis of a person's day-to-day pattern of living expressed as activities, interests, and opinions
   (D) an analysis of geographic areas for competitive study
   (E) Only (A) and (C) are correct

72. A reference group may influence one's purchases because

    (A) they are members of the same social class
    (B) they are part of middle-class America
    (C) people make comparisons between themselves and others, or try to imitate other's behavior or purchase decisions
    (D) having a mink coat is considered a status symbol
    (E) an opinion leader is a person who influences others in the group

73. Which of the following statements about personal selling is (are) true?

    (A) There should be a desire to combine mass selling and sales promotion with personal selling.
    (B) It has flexibility.
    (C) It is direct spoken communication between buyer and seller.
    (D) It is expensive, especially per contact.
    (E) All of the above.

74. Sending out unsolicited e-mail ads is referred to as

    (A) viral marketing
    (B) personalized marketing
    (C) publicity
    (D) spamming
    (E) brand equity

75. It is MOST difficult to measure the response rate in

    (A) coupon redemptions
    (B) billboard advertisements
    (C) Internet inquiries
    (D) direct mail responses
    (E) telemarketing

76. Regarding direct marketing programs, which of the following statements is TRUE?

    (A) They bypass wholesalers.
    (B) They target a general audience.
    (C) They are being used less frequently than in the past decade due to changes in technology.
    (D) They rely solely on postal mail.
    (E) They include newspaper and magazine advertising.

77. A Hispanic fiesta funded by a food company is an example of

(A) sponsorship marketing
(B) cause-related marketing
(C) green marketing
(D) event marketing
(E) guerrilla marketing

78. A local race car driver who displays advertising on his car is involved in

(A) cause-related marketing
(B) mobile marketing
(C) sponsorship marketing
(D) event marketing
(E) green marketing

79. Consider the following scenario. A company's sales force workload is 60,000 calls per year; the average salesperson can make 1,000 calls per year. Using the workload approach, how many salespeople does the company need?

(A) 60
(B) 50
(C) 55
(D) 10
(E) 600

80. During the market introduction phase of the product life cycle, the basic promotional objective is informing. If the product is a really new idea, the promotion needs to develop and build demand. This demand is known as

(A) final demand
(B) primary demand
(C) secondary demand
(D) tertiary demand
(E) selective demand

81. Which of the following is the best response for the statement, "Anyone seeking a profit maximization objective will charge high prices"?

(A) This is always true.
(B) This is not always true.
(C) Prices will always be higher than the competitor's.
(D) Prices tend to stay below the competitor's prices.
(E) None of the above relate to the statement.

82. A key point regarding sales-oriented objectives is

    (A) a larger market share, if gained at too low a price, may lead to a success with no profits
    (B) aggressive companies often aim to increase market share
    (C) larger sales volume, by itself, does not necessarily lead to higher profits
    (D) it is never easy to measure a firm's market share when determining if there is profit maximization
    (E) All of the above are correct

83. The type of price policy that tries to sell the top of the demand curve utilizing a high price, before aiming at more price-sensitive consumers, is called

    (A) skimming pricing
    (B) flexible pricing
    (C) one-price policy
    (D) penetration pricing
    (E) odd/even pricing

84. Which of the following discounts refer to a list price reduction given to channel members for the specific jobs they are doing for the manufacturer or producer?

    (A) Quantity discounts
    (B) Cash discounts
    (C) Trade discounts
    (D) Cumulative quantity discounts
    (E) Seasonal discounts

85. Which of the following terms allows a buyer to take a 4 percent discount off the face value of the invoice if the invoice is paid within 20 days, and if not, the full face value of the invoice becomes due in 60 days?

    (A) 20/60, net 4
    (B) 2/10, net 60
    (C) 2/10, net 30
    (D) 10/4, net 60
    (E) 4/20, net 60

86. Which of the following makes illegal selling the same products to different buyers at different prices?

   (A) Wheeler Lea Amendment
   (B) Unfair Trade Practice Acts
   (C) Robinson-Patman Act
   (D) Magnuson-Moss Act
   (E) Lanham Act

87. Price fixing falls under which act or amendment?

   (A) Robinson-Patman Act
   (B) Wheeler Lea Amendment
   (C) Sherman Act
   (D) Unfair Trade Practice Acts
   (E) Lanham Act

88. According to the U.S. Census Bureau, wholesalers are defined as those who sell to

   (A) retailers and other merchants
   (B) industrial users
   (C) institutional users
   (D) commercial users
   (E) All of the above

89. The most risky and challenging marketing opportunities involve

   (A) product development
   (B) diversification
   (C) market penetration
   (D) market development
   (E) All of the above are equally risky

90. Which of the following activities do wholesalers perform?

   (A) Store inventory
   (B) Supply capital
   (C) Reduce credit risk
   (D) Provide market information
   (E) All of the above

91. Marine-Unlimited buys tropical fish from local fish growers. The company takes title to the tropical fish for some period of time before selling to the many pet shops around the area on a cash or credit basis. Marine Unlimited is called a

    (A) cash-and-carry wholesaler
    (B) rack jobber
    (C) producers' cooperative
    (D) mail-order wholesaler
    (E) merchant wholesaler

92. Service wholesalers provide all the wholesaling functions. Service wholesalers include

    (A) general merchandise wholesaler
    (B) single-line (general-line) wholesaler
    (C) specialty wholesaler
    (D) All of the above
    (E) None of the above

93. A service wholesaler that carries a wide variety of nonperishable items such as hardware, electrical supplies, furniture, drugs, etc., is called a

    (A) single-line wholesaler
    (B) general merchandise wholesaler
    (C) specialty wholesaler
    (D) rack jobber
    (E) limited-function wholesaler

94. Market segmentation

    (A) assumes that most markets can be satisfied by the same marketing mix
    (B) is the same thing as positioning
    (C) tries to identify homogeneous submarkets within a larger market
    (D) means the same thing as marketing mix
    (E) identifies homogeneous and heterogeneous submarkets

95. Some of the features of cash-and-carry wholesalers include

   (A) catering to retailers too small to be served profitably by service wholesalers
   (B) accepting only cash
   (C) delivering products that they stock in their own trucks
   (D) taking title to the products they sell, but not actually handling stocking or delivering them
   (E) Both (A) and (B)

96. Sylvia Garcia brings buyers and sellers together. She is called a

   (A) selling agent
   (B) commission merchant
   (C) broker
   (D) manufacturers' agent
   (E) rack jobber

97. ABC Company segmented its broad product market and decided to target two segments, offering each segment a different marketing mix. Which approach is ABC Company following?

   (A) Differentiated segmentation
   (B) Concentrated segmentation
   (C) Mass marketing
   (D) Green marketing
   (E) Societal marketing

98. The "law of diminishing returns" states that

   (A) the demand for any product will tend to decline over time
   (B) the more of a product a person buys, the less utility that particular product offers him
   (C) if the price of a product is lowered, a smaller quantity will be demanded
   (D) if the price of a product is lowered, quantity demanded stays the same
   (E) if the price of a product is raised, a smaller quantity will be demanded

99. Annie loves her Guess jeans. She wants another pair of Guess jeans, but if there is a brand that has a lower price with similar quality, she will buy that pair instead. This is an example of

    (A) brand recognition
    (B) brand preference
    (C) brand insistence
    (D) nonrecognition
    (E) None of the above

100. Kenmore appliances (sold by Sears) are an example of a(n)

    (A) dealer brand
    (B) manufacturers' brand
    (C) licensed brand
    (D) individual brand
    (E) family brand

PRACTICE TEST 2

Answer Key

1.	(C)	35.	(D)	69.	(E)
2.	(C)	36.	(C)	70.	(C)
3.	(D)	37.	(B)	71.	(E)
4.	(D)	38.	(A)	72.	(C)
5.	(D)	39.	(C)	73.	(E)
6.	(B)	40.	(E)	74.	(D)
7.	(C)	41.	(B)	75.	(B)
8.	(E)	42.	(A)	76.	(A)
9.	(E)	43.	(A)	77.	(D)
10.	(E)	44.	(E)	78.	(C)
11.	(E)	45.	(E)	79.	(A)
12.	(A)	46.	(D)	80.	(B)
13.	(B)	47.	(B)	81.	(B)
14.	(A)	48.	(E)	82.	(C)
15.	(A)	49.	(C)	83.	(A)
16.	(B)	50.	(B)	84.	(C)
17.	(D)	51.	(B)	85.	(E)
18.	(D)	52.	(E)	86.	(C)
19.	(A)	53.	(C)	87.	(C)
20.	(D)	54.	(D)	88.	(E)
21.	(E)	55.	(A)	89.	(B)
22.	(B)	56.	(C)	90.	(E)
23.	(D)	57.	(B)	91.	(E)
24.	(E)	58.	(B)	92.	(D)
25.	(B)	59.	(A)	93.	(B)
26.	(A)	60.	(E)	94.	(C)
27.	(B)	61.	(B)	95.	(E)
28.	(B)	62.	(E)	96.	(C)
29.	(D)	63.	(D)	97.	(A)
30.	(C)	64.	(A)	98.	(E)
31.	(E)	65.	(D)	99.	(B)
32.	(D)	66.	(C)	100.	(E)
33.	(D)	67.	(B)		
34.	(E)	68.	(E)		

PRACTICE TEST 2

Detailed Explanations of Answers

1. **(C)** When one wants to calculate the markup of a product, at retail, the correct formula is Amount of Markup = Selling Price − Cost. Thus, (C) is correct. (A), (B), and (D) are incorrect formulas and won't yield the markup. (E) is incorrect because the answer is available from the given data.

2. **(C)** When trying to find the markup based upon selling price, the formula to use is Amount of Markup = Selling Price − Cost. In this example, since the selling price is $2,000 and the cost is $800, the answer is $1,200. (A), (B), (D), and (E) are incorrect calculations.

3. **(D)** In order to calculate percent of markup to selling price one would use the formula amount of markup/selling price = percent of markup to selling price. Since this comes out to 60%, (D) is correct. (A) is incorrect because $600/1,000 = 60\%$. (B), (C), and (E) are also incorrect for the same reason.

4. **(D)** Their selling price should be $1,000. (A) is incorrect because this gives a 60% markup as a percentage of the $400 cost. (B) cannot be correct because $350 is below cost, thus MOLE would be selling at a loss. (C) is incorrect because in order to calculate selling price, the formula to utilize is SP = COST + MARKUP (SP = C + M). Since the cost of $400 + 60%(SP) is not $750, this choice is wrong. (E) is also incorrect because the cost plus 60% of the selling price does not equal $5,300.

5. **(D)** The cost would be $400. (A) is incorrect; the cost will not be equal to or in excess of the selling price. (B) is incorrect; $600 is 60% × $1,000. (C) is incorrect because this is the markup percentage on cost of 60%. (E) is incorrect because Cost = Selling Price − Markup (C = SP − M). Thus, $1,000 − 60\%(1,000) = 400$, and the cost of the product was $400.

6. **(B)** The cost is $400, and the selling price is $500. (A) is incorrect since the selling price and cost can be calculated. (C) is incorrect since Markup % on Selling Price × Selling Price = Amount of Markup. When calculated, the answer is C = $400 and SP = $500; thus, (D) is also wrong. (E) is incorrect. If the amount of markup is $100, and the markup percent on selling price is $120, this answer cannot possibly be right.

7. **(C)** When figuring markup based upon cost, Selling Price = Cost + Markup. Since $200 = $150 + $50, (A), (B), (D), and (E) are all incorrect. Utilizing the formula, $200 − $150 = $50. Remember, this is the markup based upon cost, NOT retail selling price.

8. **(E)** Positioning is giving a product a specific image that differentiates it from its competition and this is done to occupy a certain place in consumers' minds in relation to competing brands. The specific positioning tool that depicts consumers' perceptions of brands is called a perceptual map or product space. Hence, (E) is the right answer.

9. **(E)** The key to remember is that this calculation is being performed on COST, not retail price. (A), $16.67, is incorrect; this would be the answer if the question had asked for a 40% markup on retail price. (B) cannot be correct because it is at cost. (C) is not correct because Selling Price = Cost + Markup. So SP = $10.00 = .4($10), or $14.00. (D) is also an incorrect answer.

10. **(E)** Positioning deals with consumers' perceptions (A). It uses a graphing tool called a perceptual map (B) or a product space diagram (C), and it sometimes incorporates consumers' ideal preferences (D). The only choice that is incorrect is (E) since positioning does not always map brands based on price and quality. The two attributes could be anything that would be relevant to the product category in question. Therefore, the correct answer is (E).

11. **(E)** The company must consider each of the elements before entering a foreign market since not doing so could result in embarrassment for the marketer (or worse). Although theme is a correct answer (A), it of itself is not sufficient to support the promotional program. Copy color (B) is important, and the impact of color for the foreign market should be studied; however, it is not the best choice. Product name (C) and the media mix (D) are also important considerations, and are correct, but by themselves they are not the best choice.

12. **(A)** The simplest step is to begin shipping out the goods. As the company gets more involved in exporting, they will create an international division to handle all of the international activities. Finally, they begin thinking of themselves as global marketers, and become a multinational organization. Answers (B), (C), and (D) are incorrect because they do not begin with the simplest step of exporting. Answer (E) is incorrect because creating an international division after becoming a multinational organization is backwards.

13. **(B)** Because of spoilage, Sugar Bear may want to utilize air. In order to increase their market and serve their customers, Sugar Bear may well want to serve the Pennsylvania market, so (A) is incorrect. Water (C) is probably unavailable between Colorado and Pennsylvania, and even if it were, the mode of transportation is probably far too slow for a perishable product. Train (D) may be a viable method of transportation, however, since the produce is a perishable product, the slower forms of transportation like train may not be the best choice for a long journey (unless refrigerated cars are used, and the customer service level is low). Pipelines (E) are not feasible options since fresh produce cannot be sent through this form of transportation.

14. **(A)** Price multiplied by quantity demanded equals total revenues. When a demand curve is inelastic, small changes in price do not cause a change in the quantity demanded. Therefore, if the price goes up, so will total revenues. Similarly, if price goes down, revenues too would decline since quantity demanded remains unchanged. In other words, when the demand is inelastic, both changes in price and revenues move in the same direction (up or down). Only (A) correctly reflects the concept of inelastic demand.

15. **(A)** Private warehousing would be the best choice. If a company stores large volumes of goods on a regular basis, they should probably use company-owned or private warehouses. Public warehouses (B) are best suited to seasonal use. (C) a distribution center's main function is to redistribute the stock, not to store it, so this would be an incorrect choice. Containerization (D) refers to the grouping of individual items into economical shipping quantities, and is incorrect. All of the above should not be utilized given the situation, so (E) is not the best choice.

16. **(B)** Critics often complain that companies intentionally sell substandard products to consumers (A) in order to make excessive profits (E). Others claim that some companies use overly aggressive sales (C) methods to "push" products onto consumers. Finally, some claim that advertising is often guilty of misleading consumers with deceptive advertising (D). The only choice that does not constitute a valid criticism of marketing is (B) and that is the right answer.

17. **(D)** This question involves selective processes when one is exposed to stimuli. With selective exposure (D) our minds and eyes seek out and notice information that interests us. In the example, rollerblade products begin to interest you, so you notice ads about them more often. Selective

retention (A) occurs when we remember only what we want to remember. This may occur after we have been exposed, suddenly, to the information. Selective perception (B) is when we screen out or modify ideas, messages, and information that conflict with previously learned attitudes and beliefs. Selective response (C) is incorrect because there is not a category called selective response. (E) is incorrect because one of the above, (D), is true.

18. **(D)** Advertising falls under promotion, which is the communication between the seller and potential buyer to influence attitudes and behavior. Product (A), price (B), and place (C) are all parts of the marketing mix, but advertising does not fit under them. Perception (E) is not one of the "4 P's" in the marketing mix.

19. **(A)** Neither the product life cycle (E) nor the BCG Matrix (D) nor market segmentation (C) nor image psychology (B) describe the way a product is perceived by customers on two important attributes. The correct answer is product positioning (A).

20. **(D)** Preemptive differentiation is defined as the process of choosing a product attribute or difference that competitors would not be able to duplicate. In essence, the firm is taking preemptive action against its competitors; hence, the right answer is (D).

21. **(E)** Pioneering advertising is usually done early in the product's life cycle and informs potential customers of the product and its benefits, generating primary demand for the category. Institutional advertising (A) promotes a specific organization, not a product. Competitive advertising (B) aims to develop customers' preference for a specific brand. Product advertising (C) aims to sell a product. Reminder advertising (D) aims to keep the product name before the public later in the product's life cycle.

22. **(B)** Geographic segmentation deals with breaking down a market based on the geographic location of consumers, so (A) is incorrect. Benefit segmentation deals with the different benefits from a product sought by consumers, so (C) is incorrect. Psychographic segmentation involves consumers' lifestyles (D) and behavioral segmentation divides a market based on usage behavior of consumers (E). Both (D) and (E) do not utilize gender, income, or occupation to segment markets, so they are incorrect choices. However, demographic segmentation (B) does take into consideration consumers' demographics such as income, occupation, and gender. Therefore, the right answer is (B).

23. **(D)** There are four branding strategies, namely line extensions, brand extensions, multibrands, and new brands. These four strategic options are contingent upon two factors: brand name (existing versus new) and product category (existing versus new). Variety seeking (E) and product extension (A) should be ruled out right at the onset since they are irrelevant to branding options. Only in the new brand option (D) does a firm concoct a new brand name for a new product category. Therefore, the correct answer is (D).

24. **(E)** Service marketing is different from product marketing in at least four ways. They are intangibility (A), inseparability (B), perishability (C), and variability (E). Homogeneity is not one of the traits of services, so (D) should be eliminated. The correct answer is (E) because variability refers to the fact that the quality of a service is contingent upon who provided the service, and when, where, and how it was provided.

25. **(B)** Before any medium is chosen, a firm must specify the target market and audience, and know their interests, habits, and behavior. Answers (A) and (D) do not have anything to do with the medium chosen. As many marketers will say, the most expensive medium (C) is not always the best if it does not target the correct audience. (E) is also incorrect, but should be researched after the target market and audience are identified.

26. **(A)** The four stages in the product life cycle (PLC) are introduction, growth, maturity, and decline in that particular order with respect to time. The introduction stage (B) is characterized by low sales and profits when the product is new in the market. This is followed by growth (C) where both sales and profits rapidly increase. Then comes maturity (A) where the product faces intense competition, sales and profits reach their peaks, and weaker competitors drop out of the market. Therefore, (A) is the right answer.

27. **(B)** Licensing a brand means giving another firm the right to a trademark and/or brand name in exchange for a yearly fee (royalty). Therefore, licensed brand (B) correctly describes Mark's brand sponsorship strategy.

28. **(B)** Concept tests usually rely on written descriptions of new products, and may be augmented with sketches of other literature. Several key questions are asked during the concept testing phase of new product development, including "How does the consumer perceive the product," and "who would use the product?" The firm would internally evaluate all new products and proposals to see if they "fit" the product strategy, so an internal test (A) is incorrect. (C) is not correct. A weighted point system (D) can establish

criteria for product screening, but does not answer the above questions. Likewise, a non-weighted point system can establish criteria, but it doesn't provide answers to the above questions, thus (E) is incorrect.

29. **(D)** Test marketing is performed to see if consumers will actually buy the product. Additionally, changes can be made to the marketing mix variables in a controlled setting. Selected controlled markets are those markets in which the total test is conducted by an outside organization or agency. The tests are conducted by paying retailers for shelf space, guaranteeing distribution to the most popular test market(s), so (A) is incorrect. (B) is not the correct answer. Store audits are conducted by groups (such as A.C. Nielsen), measuring sales in grocery stores and the number of cases ordered by the stores. Standard markets (C) is also incorrect because standard markets are those test sites where companies sell a new product through normal channels, and then monitor the results. (E) is incorrect because there is a correct choice.

30. **(C)** The final phase of the new product planning process is known as commercialization. This is when the product is positioned in the marketplace and launched. (A) is incorrect because prototype development occurs in the development phase. The market testing phase (B) of the new product development process involves exposing the actual product to consumers under realistic, yet somewhat controlled, conditions. The new product's niche (D) is defined during the initial strategic phase of the new product development cycle. Finally, (E) is not correct, because there is a correct answer.

31. **(E)** Support goods are those goods used to assist in producing other goods and services. Support goods may include services, supplies, installations, and accessory equipment, thus all of the above are correct. (A), (B), (C), and (D) are all examples of support goods, thus each are incorrect choices.

32. **(D)** Form utility deals with something that is made out of some other material(s), usually called raw materials, thus the manufacturing of a telephone creates form utility. Task utility (A) is incorrect because this is service-related and deals with a person providing a task for someone. (B) is incorrect because possession utility refers to having the right to use or consume a good or service. Time utility is having a product ready for the customer(s) when she or he needs or wants it, so (C) is incorrect. Place utility (E) refers to having a product for a customer where they want it, thus (E) is incorrect.

33. **(D)** All of the above functions must be performed. The buying function (A) is the purchase of products or services, and is essential in macro-marketing. Likewise, transportation (B) is a required function of macro-marketing, and includes physically moving products to various locations within a channel of distribution. Marketing information (C) is the communication function performed in macro-marketing and is one of the eight universal functions that marketers perform. All three of these answers help make up the eight universal functions of marketing performed in a macro-marketing environment. (E) is incorrect because all are universal macro-marketing functions.

34. **(E)** The marketing company era saw the development of the marketing concept that states that marketers should strive to satisfy consumer wants and needs, *at a profit!* (A) is incorrect because the marketing concept was not developed or practiced during this era. (B) is incorrect. During the marketing department era, all marketing functions were brought together under one department, but this was not a company-wide practice. (C) is incorrect because during the production era no consideration was given to the market or what customers wanted. (D) is incorrect. During the sales era, a company stresses selling over marketing because of the increase in competition.

35. **(D)** Forming heterogeneous markets is the opposite of what one wants to do in the development of product-market segments. The marketer, or product manager, should be looking for homogeneous market segments. (A) is incorrect. The marketer should strive to find a name for the possible segments. (B) is also incorrect because the marketer should list the potential customer needs (as well as wants) for each of the segments. (C) is incorrect because the marketer needs to know the approximate size of the market in order to assure profitability. Since (D) is a correct choice, (E) is incorrect.

36. **(C)** Product development deals with offering *new* or *improved* products for current or present markets; thus, (C) is correct. (A) is incorrect because American Express is trying to penetrate the market by attempting to increase current product usage. (B) is not correct because Taco Bell is expanding its market with a current product and are therefore attempting market development. (D) is incorrect because Nintendo is taking a whole new product into an entirely new market or attempting new venture strategies. (E) is not the best choice because there is a correct answer.

37. **(B)** Straight rebuy is a routine purchase of an item that is commonly purchased. (A) is not correct because new task buying occurs when an organization has a new need and the buyer wants a great deal of information

about the product prior to purchase. (C) is also incorrect. Modified rebuy is the in-between process of buying where some review is done, although not as much as in a new-task buying situation. Purchase (D) is incorrect because the question relates to a repurchase. (E) is incorrect, because there is a correct answer.

38. **(A)** People who specialize in buying are called purchasing agents. (B) is the manager in the marketing area who is concerned with personal selling. Order takers (C) are salespeople who get orders from, or sell to, the regular or "typical" customer. Order getters (D) are salespeople who specialize in generating new business. Finally, any of the above (E) is incorrect. There is only one most correct choice.

39. **(C)** Vendor analysis is the process used to evaluate suppliers and how they are working out for the company. An evaluation (A) is not the most correct answer. An evaluation is less formal and not as detailed as a vendor analysis. A checklist (B) may be part of a vendor analysis but more information is needed to make an assessment of the vendor than is provided for in a checklist, so this answer is incorrect. Subjective interpretation (D) may be used in analyzing the vendor, but objective measurement is also needed, making this a poor choice. Buyer analysis (E) could be performed by the vendor, but is not needed by the buyer analyzing the vendor. Therefore, this answer is not correct.

40. **(E)** Many people are involved in certain purchase decisions. All of the people listed could have a possible buying influence through the concept of multiple buying influences. Users (A) is a correct choice, however, not the most correct, since all of the individuals listed may have an influence on the final purchase decision. Buyers (B) are those involved in the purchase process; however, the process may have been initiated by a user or someone else. Thus, even though by itself this would be correct, it is not the best answer. Influencers (C) are those that influence the purchase decision and may share in the purchase decision; however, this is not the most correct answer. Gatekeepers (D) may also be influencers, such as secretaries and other administrative assistants; however, this is not the most correct choice.

41. **(B)** Every item should be inspected if nonstandardized products have been ordered. (A) is not correct because negotiated contract buying is agreeing to a contract that allows for changes in the purchase agreement. (C) is also incorrect; sampling buying means looking at only a small part of the potential purchase, and would not be the best method of purchase in

this situation. Description buying (D) is the purchase of a product based on a verbal or written description. A routine response buying situation (E) is where the purchaser is making a normal purchase of products purchased before, and should not be used in this situation.

42. **(A)** Defining the problem is the first step that should be undertaken. Solving the problem (B) is the final step that should be undertaken, and is thus incorrect. Collecting problem-specific data (C) cannot be undertaken until the problem is defined. Analyzing the situation (D) is the second step, and therefore is incorrect. Defining a sample (E) shouldn't be undertaken until after the situation has been analyzed.

43. **(A)** Trying to ascertain what the problem is takes the majority of time in the process. (B) is incorrect. Although situational analysis may be time consuming, it does not take as much time as problem definition, and rarely would it require as much as half of the research time. Data collection (C) is timeconsuming but does not take as much time as problem definition. Problem solving (D) takes place after data collection, and usually doesn't require the time and effort that the other phases do; thus, it is incorrect. The development of alternative solutions (E) again takes time, but the problem definition takes the most time, and in a lot of cases, takes well over half the research time. Therefore, (E) is incorrect.

44. **(E)** A research proposal is a plan that specifies what information is needed and how it will be obtained. In addition, most proposals have information as to the cost of the data collection. (A) is incorrect. A research proposal is stated after the situational analysis, not after the problem definition. (B) is a definition of a research proposal and is included in the body of the proposal, but is not the best answer. (C) usually is part of the research proposal, but is not the best answer. (D) is incorrect because both (A) and (C) are NOT correct.

45. **(E)** All survey results require care in result interpretation. The researcher should be trained in this area. (A), (B), (C), and (D) all require care but are not the best answers for the question. Each must be analyzed carefully and the results accurately stated with care.

46. **(D)** Research is needed to help keep marketing managers in touch with their markets. (A) is incorrect, because research should be planned by both specialists and marketing managers to make sure the user's needs are being met. (B) is incorrect because marketing research is much more than just survey design and statistics. (C) is incorrect. Marketing research is used

by everyone involved in the marketing process. (E) is incorrect. Marketing research should be an on-going process.

47. **(B)**   Primary data, while costly to acquire, does have a number of big pluses, including the provision of fresh market information (A), providing a level of secrecy from competitors' prying eyes (C), fitting the company's marketing needs snugly (D), and rapid information acquisition. Taken together, the considerable advantages of collecting primary data need to be weighed against the initial high acquisition cost.

48. **(E)**   The U.S. birthrate is starting to drop now with more couples waiting longer to have children and more women entering the work force, and there is less of a want for larger families. (A) is true but is not the best choice because (D) is also correct. (B) is incorrect. The only time the birthrate rose sharply due to returning soldiers was during the post-World War II "baby boom," which lasted about 15 years into the early 1960s. (C) is incorrect because the birthrate is simply not rising sharply. This is affected by the fact that there is not an abundance of women at the childbearing age. (D) is true, but not the best answer because (A) is also correct.

49. **(C)**   The United States does have the highest divorce rate in the world—about 38% of the marriages in the U.S. end in divorce. England has nothing to do with divorce rates in the United States. Their divorce rate is lower than the U.S. rate; thus, (A) is incorrect. (B) is incorrect. The U.S. does not have the lowest divorce rate in the world; the opposite is true. (D) is also incorrect. Not only does England not have the lowest divorce rate, but the percentage given is incorrect. The United States does not have a divorce rate of 13%, it is closer to 38%; thus, (E) is not the most correct choice.

50. **(B)**   The economy's gross domestic product (GDP) is a widely available measure of the output of the whole economy and the total market value of goods and services for the United States (produced in a year). The economic system (A) is the way an economy organizes to use scarce resources to produce the goods and services and then distribute them to society for consumption; thus, (A) is incorrect. Gross sales (C) is the total amount charged to all customers during a given time period, and is incorrect. Gross margin (D) refers to businesses and the money they have to cover expenses of selling and other business operations. (E) is incorrect. The term used to be used to define the output of the economy, but was dropped in favor of gross domestic product.

51. **(B)** Disposable income is the income left after paying taxes, which is used to make necessary expenditures such as housing and car payments. (A) refers to business transactions and is the money left over, for a business, to cover the expenses associated with running that business (i.e., sales expenses and operating expenses) and is incorrect. (C) is also incorrect. Net profit is what a company has earned from their operations during a specified time period. Discretionary income (D) is that income left over after taxes and after payments for necessities, so it is incorrect. Family income (E) is money that the family, or household, earns and is incorrect.

52. **(E)** Advertising, publicity, and personal selling are promotion activities and are not a form of sales promotion; thus, sales promotion would not include those activities. Advertising (A) is part of the promotion mix; however, it is not the best choice of those given, and thus is incorrect. (B) is also incorrect; although it is a promotion mix, it is not part of sales promotion. (C) is also incorrect, because it is not the best choice of those given. Point-of-purchase materials (D) would be a form of sales promotion used to stimulate interest, trial, and purchase of products at the point-of-sale; therefore, it is incorrect.

53. **(C)** The primary users of the Internet today are Gen X and college students (D). The use of e-mail is growing (A) and B2B advertising is fast growing on the Internet (B). Internet marketing does allow buyers to learn more about sellers (E). Therefore, all the above statements are true. However, the statement that says that the primary users of the Internet are baby boomers (C) is false, which makes it the right response to this question.

54. **(D)** Raising prices in this situation would most likely boost your competitor's position and reduce your customer base. Meeting competition (A) would be likely with a status quo objective and is incorrect. (B) is also incorrect because maintaining stable prices may discourage price competition and leave the situation in the status quo. (C) should not be selected because the manager utilizing a status quo objective does want to avoid price competition. Finally, (E) is incorrect because it's a promotional function that would not be used in a status quo situation.

55. **(A)** Decoding is the process that the receiver uses to translate the seller's message, and is a correct choice. Encoding (B) is how the seller translates ideas and thoughts about selling the product into words and/or symbols and is an incorrect choice. Noise (C) is incorrect. Noise refers to those distractions in the environment that may create an error in the communication

process. (D) refers to the sender, or the seller, of the message and is not a correct choice. Finally, (E) is the potential consumer, not how the message is translated, so it too is incorrect.

56. **(C)** Both the early and late majority(s) make up approximately 34% (per group) of the adopting public. Innovators (A) make up around 2½% of the adopting public, so this is incorrect. Early adopters (B) make up around 12% of the adopting public and is not the most correct answer. The late majority (D), as stated before, makes up about 34% of the adopting public and would be one of two groups who represent the largest adoption percentage; however, this is not the most correct choice. The laggards (E) represent anywhere from 5 to 16% of the adopting public, if they adopt at all. This is an incorrect choice.

57. **(B)** Pulling is getting the consumers to ask the intermediaries for products, thus forcing these channel members to request the product from the manufacturers. (A) is the process of "pushing" a product through the distribution channel and is incorrect. (C) is a type of internal marketing done to get the employees involved in selling specific products, so it is incorrect. (D) is incorrect. There is not one correct promotion mix for all selling situations. (E) is generally used when the intermediaries do not want to help, or cooperate, with the manufacturers.

58. **(B)** In this stage, promotion emphasis shifts from trying to create primary demand to that of selective demand. The main objective is to convince consumers that the company's brand is the best choice for purchase. Market introduction (A) would have a promotion emphasis on building primary demand, not selective, and is incorrect. Market maturity (C) utilizes reminder advertising and promotion about the company's brand, and is not the most correct choice. Sales decline (D) utilizes targeted promotions for specific segments, or targets of the brand, and so is incorrect. Competition decline (E) refers to the fact that the competition is leaving the market, so it is incorrect. Competition decline is not one of the phases of the product life cycle.

59. **(A)** Banners and streamers are examples of sales promotions aimed at the final consumer or end user to stimulate trial of the brand or product. (B) is an example of a sales promotion activity aimed at the intermediary and is not correct. (C) also is aimed toward intermediaries, trying to induce the middlemen to pay special attention to a particular product or brand, thus increasing sales. It is incorrect. Bonuses (D) are an internal sales promotion

activity that attempts to motivate the company's own sales force. It is incorrect. (E) is incorrect; training materials are used as an internal method of sales promotion aimed at sales people, so that they pay particular attention to a given product or brand.

60. **(E)**   Because of the flexibility of trucks, around 75 percent of all physical products transported by the producer to the end user travel by truck. (A), (B), (C), and (D) are simply incorrect choices, forcing the student to think about how the products they purchase are received and stocked by retailers and other merchants. Although somewhat expensive, products could not reach their final destination if it weren't for trucks.

61. **(B)**   In this question, it states that the firm's total revenues decline when price goes up by $5. That means the quantity demanded must have declined substantially in response to the price increase for total revenues to drop (Price × Quantity Demanded = Total Revenues). This is characteristic of elastic demand curves. Hence, the right answer is (B).

62. **(E)**   Some of the assumptions of pure or perfect competition are that there are many buyers and sellers in the market (A), there is perfect information in the market (B), the product being sold is homogeneous among the many sellers (C), and there is little or no entry or exit barriers (D). Since all these assumptions are true, the correct answer is "all of the above" (E).

63. **(D)**   Storing is the marketing function of holding goods. Storing provides time utility for the firm and its customers. If consumption does not match production, storing is necessary. The storing of goods allows producers to achieve economies of scale for their products, helping to keep prices down. (A) is true, but not the correct choice. (B) is also true, but again not the most correct answer. (C) is also true, but not the correct answer. None of the above (E) cannot be true since all of the above are in fact ways to alternate or vary the firm's marketing mix.

64. **(A)**   Time utility is provided by storing, and is thus the correct choice. Goods must be ready when they are needed, wanted, or demanded by the consumer or else the firm loses sales. Place utility (B) is not achieved. Storage of goods at warehouses does not provide the consumer with a readily available product. Since the consumer does not get the possession of the product through the storage function, possession utility (C) is incorrect, as is ownership utility (D). All of the above are not correct, so (E) is incorrect.

65. **(D)** This question relates to the four types of growth opportunities that firms may pursue. Product development (A) is marketing new products for existing customers. Since the WSJ is trying to attract new customers, (A) is incorrect. Diversification (B) is marketing new products to new markets. Since WSJ hasn't changed its "product," (B) is incorrect. Market penetration (C) is a growth strategy that involves selling existing products in existing markets, so this too is incorrect. Target marketing (E) is incorrect since it is too broad and doesn't specifically address the situation described in the question. The correct answer is market development (D), since it involves selling existing products (WSJ) in new markets (student population).

66. **(C)** To offset the shortcomings of low speed and high cost, and still get business from small shippers, railroads allow groups of shippers to pool like goods into a full car. This is termed *pool car service*. Containerization (A) is incorrect. It refers to the grouping of individual items into economical shipping quantities. Piggyback service (B) refers to the loading of truck trailers onto railroad cars for transportation and is incorrect. Diversion in transit (D) is also incorrect. This refers to the redirection of carloads already in transit. Birdyback service (E) refers to loading trucks or trailers onto airplanes for faster transport to their place of destination. This answer is also incorrect.

67. **(B)** A tariff, by definition, is a tax imposed on imports (B). Therefore, this is the correct answer. A quota is a quantitative restriction on the amount of goods that can be imported from a country (A). A boycott is defined as a total ban on imports (C). Franchising is defined as a mode of entering foreign markets through licensing arrangements (D). Finally, (E) is incorrect because it too discusses a boycott rather than a tariff.

68. **(E)** When striving to satisfy basic human needs such as accomplishment, fun, relaxation, and others as stated in the other answers, individuals would find themselves in both the self-esteem needs level and the love and belongingness needs level of the hierarchy. Physiological needs (A) are needs for food, drink, rest, and sex. Safety needs (B) are needs for protection or well-being. Self-actualization (C) is also incorrect. This needs level refers to people who strive for total fulfillment of their maximum capabilities, and is only reached by a small portion of the population. Love and belongingness (D) is a good answer; however, it is not the best choice.

69. **(E)** Selective retention, selective perception, and selective exposure all comprise the selective processes. Selective retention (A) means that we remember only what we want to remember, and is true, but is not the most

correct response. Selective perception (B) refers to the fact that we screen out ideas, or modify those ideas and messages that conflict with what we have already learned and with our beliefs, and is true, but not the most correct response. Selective exposure (C) means that our eyes and minds seek out and notice only what interests us; we selectively expose ourselves to our environment. However, it is not the most correct answer. Selective response (D) is fictitious. A response, however, is an effort to satisfy a need. This is an incorrect answer.

70. **(C)** Countertrade is a form of market exchange in international business that need not involve the use of money. Bartering is the oldest and simplest form of countertrade. Therefore, (C) is the right choice. Countertrade is definitely not an illegal activity in the U.S. (A). It is practiced in planned as well as market-oriented economies, so (B) is false. (D) is false because subsistence economies are by definition self-sufficient so they do not engage in any form of trade. Finally, (E) is false since it claims that both (B) and (D) are true.

71. **(E)** Both lifestyle analyses and an analysis of a person's day-today living are referred to as psychographics. (A) is a true statement, but is not the best answer. (B) is totally made up and therefore incorrect. This is not a definition of a psychographic. (C) is true, but not the best choice. (D) refers to geographics, or locations of consumers.

72. **(C)** A reference group may influence one's purchase behavior because people make comparisons between themselves and others. Reference groups are the social, economic, or professional groups an individual uses to evaluate their opinions or beliefs. A social class (A) is a group of people who have approximately equal social position as viewed by society. (B) is not relevant to the question at hand and is incorrect. (D) may be a status symbol, but this has no bearing on the question, so it is incorrect. An opinion leader (E) may be part of a reference group, but this refers to an individual rather than a group.

73. **(E)** All of the statements reflect personal selling and are true. Personal selling is part of the promotional mix of marketing. In order to make it more effective, there should be a desire to combine aspects of advertising and sales promotion (A), although this is not the most correct response. Personal selling is the most flexible (B) of all of the promotion variables; however, this is not the most correct response. (C) is true, however, not the most correct response. Personal selling is expensive (D), especially per

contact, and this is one of the reasons it should be combined with the other promotional mix variables. This, however, is not the best response.

74. **(D)**   Spamming (D) is the term given to sending out unsolicited e-mail en masse.

75. **(B)**   Measuring the response rate of a promotion campaign is an important aspect of a firm's overall promotion strategy. The task of measurement is relatively easier in the case of direct marketing compared to media advertising. Coupon redemptions (A), Internet inquiries (C), direct-mail responses (D), and telemarketing (E) are various forms of direct marketing. However, billboard ads (B) are not part of a direct marketing campaign. As such, it is difficult to measure the effectiveness of a billboard ad and that is the best response to this question.

76. **(A)**   Direct-marketing programs are witnessing robust growth in the current years, so (C) is incorrect. One of the reasons why firms are switching from media advertising to direct marketing is because direct marketing targets a specific audience, thus reducing "waste." That rules out (B). (D) is also false since direct marketing media encompasses a variety of options including e-mail, telemarketing, and postal mail; however, it does not include newspaper and magazine advertising (E). The only true statement is the fact that direct marketing bypasses middlemen such as wholesalers (A).

77. **(D)**   A Hispanic fiesta event funded by a food company is an example of event marketing (D). Thus, (D) is the right answer. The only other choice that may have come close to the right answer is sponsorship marketing (A). However, there is no evidence in the question to indicate that the food company is promoting its name during the fiesta, so (A) ought to be ruled out. Cause-related marketing programs involve a partnership between profit and non-profit organizations to benefit a social cause. Since there is no evidence of a social cause in this question, (B) is incorrect. Green marketing is environmentally friendly marketing practices. There is no indication of this in the question, so (C) is incorrect. Finally, (E) is untrue because there is no evidence of covert guerilla marketing tactics being used in this question.

78. **(C)**   This is a clear case of sponsorship marketing (C), which happens to be the right answer. In sponsorship marketing, a firm usually pays a celebrity to display the corporate name and/or logo usually on their apparel or automobile in order to give the firm added advertising mileage. In this

question, that is what the race car driver (celebrity) is doing on behalf of his/her "sponsor."

79. **(A)**   A simple arithmetic question. The total sales workload is 60,000 calls per year. One salesperson on average can make 1,000 calls per year. Therefore, in order to find out how many salespeople are needed to cover the entire workload, one will have to divide 60,000 by 1,000. The correct answer is 60 (60,000/1,000).

80. **(B)**   Primary demand is building demand for an entire product category (i.e., coffee) rather than a specific brand (i.e., Maxwell House). (A) is incorrect because final demand does not exist. Secondary demand (C) is also incorrect for the same reason. Tertiary demand (D) is another fictitious term and is incorrect. Selective demand (E) is creating demand for a specific brand rather than an entire product category, and does not fit as an answer for this particular question.

81. **(B)**   Pricing to achieve maximization of profits does not always lead to higher prices. Demand and supply may bring high prices if the competition cannot offer a good substitute product. (A) is incorrect. High prices are not always charged in order to develop profit maximization. (C) and (D) are incorrect because the price of competition is usually developed based upon the elasticity of price for a given product or market. (E) is not the correct choice, because one of the other answers is correct.

82. **(C)**   Larger sales volumes do not necessarily lead to higher profits for a company. (A) and (B) may be objectives but are too vague, and are incorrect in reference to sales-oriented objectives. (D) is incorrect. It would be a correct answer if it read "…usually easier to measure a firm's market share…" rather than "…never easier…." (E) is incorrect because all of the other answers are not true.

83. **(A)**   With the introduction of every new product, there is a group of consumers willing to pay premium prices to try it. This provides an opportunity to launch the product at higher prices before competition forces the prices down. The skimming policy attempts to "skim the cream" off of the top of the market, thus recouping research and development costs early on prior to reducing the price for the rest of the market. Flexible pricing (B) refers to offering different prices to different customers, and is incorrect. One-price policies (C) are policies that offer products to the customers for the same price. Penetration pricing (D) refers to offering the product to the market with an initial low price, and is the opposite of skimming. Odd/

even pricing (E) is a form of psychological pricing, setting prices with odd or even endings depending on consumer perception, and is an incorrect response.

84. **(C)** Trade discounts, also known as functional discounts, are given for various activities performed by the channel member for the producer. Quantity discounts (A) are given to encourage volume purchases. Cash discounts (B) are given to encourage buyers to pay their bills early. Cumulative quantity discounts (D) are give to encourage volume purchases like quantity discounts, but allow the purchaser to buy products at different times until they have accumulated enough in purchases to qualify for a volume discount. Seasonal discounts (E) are given to encourage buyers to purchase products early, and out-of-season, to free up space for the manufacturer, among other reasons.

85. **(E)** This billing method is utilized by producers to encourage the early payment of invoices. It helps to increase cash flow for the manufacturer or producer. Most buyers take advantage of these types of terms because it allows a substantial savings on the purchase. (A), (B), (C), and (D) are different terms allowing for different discounts. They may not even make sense, and are thus incorrect choices.

86. **(C)** The Robinson-Patman Act makes it illegal to sell the same products to different buyers at different prices; therefore, (C) is the correct choice. The Wheeler Lea Amendment (A) bans unfair or deceptive acts in commerce. The Unfair Trade Practice Acts (B) puts a lower limit on prices. The Magnuson-Moss Act (D) is a law requiring that producers provide a clearly written warranty for consumer products. The Lanham Act (E) prohibits a company from misrepresenting another companies' products.

87. **(C)** The Sherman Act covers price fixing; therefore, (C) is the correct answer. The Robinson-Patman Act (A) makes it illegal to sell the same products to different buyers at different prices. The Wheeler Lea Amendment (B) bans unfair or deceptive acts in commerce. The Unfair Trade Practice Acts (D) put a lower limit on prices. The Lanham Act (E) prohibits a company from misrepresenting another companies' products.

88. **(E)** The U.S. Bureau of the Census defines wholesaling as concerned with activities of those persons or establishments that sell to retailers and other merchants (A), and/or to industrial (B), institutional (C), and commercial (D) users. Therefore, (E) is the correct answer.

89. **(B)** Among the four types of growth opportunities described in the question, diversification (B) would be most risky because it involves marketing new products in new markets. In other words, both the product and market are brand new in the case of diversification and that increases the uncertainty level along with risk.

90. **(E)** Wholesalers can store inventory (A) to reduce a producer's need to carry large stocks, thus cutting the producer's warehousing expenses; supply capital (B) to reduce a producer's need for working capital by buying the producer's output and carrying it in inventory until it is sold; reduce credit risk (C) by selling to customers the wholesaler knows and taking the loss if these customers do not pay; and provide market information (D) as an informed buyer and seller closer to the market. The wholesaler reduces the producer's need for market research. All of the above (E) is the correct answer.

91. **(E)** Merchant wholesalers own (take title to) the products they sell. Cash-and-carry wholesalers (A) operate as service wholesalers, except that the customer must pay cash. Rack jobbers (B) specialize in nonfood products sold through grocery stores and supermarkets, often displayed on wire racks owned by the rack jobber. Producers' cooperatives (C) operate almost as full-service wholesalers with the profits going to the cooperative's customer members. Mail-order wholesalers (D) sell out of a catalog that may be distributed widely to smaller industrial customers or retailers who might not be called on by other middlemen.

92. **(D)** Service wholesalers can be broken down into general merchandise wholesalers (A), single-line (general-line) wholesalers (B), or specialty wholesalers (C). The correct answer is (D).

93. **(B)** General merchandise wholesalers originally developed to serve the early retailers such as general stores, which carry a wide variety of non-perishable items. Single-line wholesalers (A) carry a narrower line of merchandise than general merchandise wholesalers. Specialty wholesalers (C) carry an even more narrow range of products and offer more information and services than other types of service wholesalers. Rack jobbers (D) specialize in nonfood products sold through grocery stores and supermarkets, often displayed on wire racks owned by the rack jobber. Limited-function wholesalers (E) provide only limited wholesaling functions.

94. **(C)** Market segmentation is the process of dividing a large, heterogeneous market comprised of consumers with diverse needs into smaller, homogeneous

submarkets (C). The notion of segmentation runs contrary to the assumption that most markets can be satisfied with the same offering (A). Segmentation may precede positioning in the overall scheme of target marketing, but they are clearly not the same thing, so (B) is false. Likewise, segmentation is not the same as a marketing mix since the latter involves the product, place, price, and promotion strategies of a firm, so (D) too is incorrect. (E) is incorrect since market segmentation actually tries to isolate homogeneous submarkets within the total heterogeneous market.

95. **(E)**   Cash-and-carry wholesalers will only accept cash (B). Some retailers, such as small auto repair shops, are too small to be served profitably by a service wholesaler, so the cash-and-carry wholesalers cater to these types of businesses on a cash basis (A). A truck wholesaler delivers products that they stock in their own trucks (C). Drop shippers take title to the products they sell, but do not handle, stock, or deliver them (D).

96. **(C)**   Brokers bring buyers and sellers together; Sylvia Garcia is a broker. Selling agents (A) are responsible for the marketing job for producers. A selling agent may handle the entire output of one or more producers. Commission merchants (B) handle products shipped to them by sellers, complete the sale, and send the money, minus their commission, to each seller. Manufacturers' agents (D) sell similar products for several non-competing producers, for a commission on what is sold. Rack jobbers (E) specialize in nonfood products sold through grocery stores and supermarkets, often displayed on wire racks owned by the rack jobber.

97. **(A)**   Differentiated segmentation takes place when a firm offers different marketing mix elements to various segments of customers just as described in this question. Therefore, (A) is the correct answer. Concentrated segmentation (B) occurs when a firm pursues just one segment of consumers with a unique marketing mix. That is not the case in this question. Mass marketing (C) is incorrect since it does not involve any segmentation at all. Green marketing (D) is environmentally friendly marketing, which has nothing to do with the question. Similarly, societal marketing (E) is a marketing philosophy that tries to balance consumers' short-term needs with societal welfare. This too is irrelevant with respect to the question, so (E) is incorrect.

98. **(E)**   The law of *diminishing returns* states that as the price of a product increases, the quantity demanded of the same product declines (E). As

such, the graph of demand versus price is a downward-sloping straight line. None of the other choices correctly depicts the law of diminishing returns.

99. **(B)** Annie prefers Guess jeans but may choose another brand if it has a lower price and similar quality. This is called brand preference. In brand recognition (A) you may not intend to purchase the product but you recognize the brand name. If Annie refused to buy any other jeans but Guess jeans, she would show brand insistence (C). Brand nonrecognition (D) is when the final consumers do not recognize a brand. Because (B) is the correct answer, (E) could not be correct.

100. **(E)** Kenmore is a family brand (brand name for several products) of Sears, so (E) is the correct choice. Dealer brands (A) such as Ace Hardware are created by middlemen. Manufacturer brands (B) are created by manufacturers and include brands such as Whirlpool, Ford, and IBM. A licensed brand (C) is a well-known brand that sellers pay to use, such as Walt Disney. An individual brand name (D) separates brand names for each product.

ANSWER SHEETS

Practice Test 1
Practice Test 2

PRACTICE TEST 1

Answer Sheet

1. Ⓐ Ⓑ Ⓒ Ⓓ Ⓔ
2. Ⓐ Ⓑ Ⓒ Ⓓ Ⓔ
3. Ⓐ Ⓑ Ⓒ Ⓓ Ⓔ
4. Ⓐ Ⓑ Ⓒ Ⓓ Ⓔ
5. Ⓐ Ⓑ Ⓒ Ⓓ Ⓔ
6. Ⓐ Ⓑ Ⓒ Ⓓ Ⓔ
7. Ⓐ Ⓑ Ⓒ Ⓓ Ⓔ
8. Ⓐ Ⓑ Ⓒ Ⓓ Ⓔ
9. Ⓐ Ⓑ Ⓒ Ⓓ Ⓔ
10. Ⓐ Ⓑ Ⓒ Ⓓ Ⓔ
11. Ⓐ Ⓑ Ⓒ Ⓓ Ⓔ
12. Ⓐ Ⓑ Ⓒ Ⓓ Ⓔ
13. Ⓐ Ⓑ Ⓒ Ⓓ Ⓔ
14. Ⓐ Ⓑ Ⓒ Ⓓ Ⓔ
15. Ⓐ Ⓑ Ⓒ Ⓓ Ⓔ
16. Ⓐ Ⓑ Ⓒ Ⓓ Ⓔ
17. Ⓐ Ⓑ Ⓒ Ⓓ Ⓔ
18. Ⓐ Ⓑ Ⓒ Ⓓ Ⓔ
19. Ⓐ Ⓑ Ⓒ Ⓓ Ⓔ
20. Ⓐ Ⓑ Ⓒ Ⓓ Ⓔ
21. Ⓐ Ⓑ Ⓒ Ⓓ Ⓔ
22. Ⓐ Ⓑ Ⓒ Ⓓ Ⓔ
23. Ⓐ Ⓑ Ⓒ Ⓓ Ⓔ
24. Ⓐ Ⓑ Ⓒ Ⓓ Ⓔ
25. Ⓐ Ⓑ Ⓒ Ⓓ Ⓔ
26. Ⓐ Ⓑ Ⓒ Ⓓ Ⓔ
27. Ⓐ Ⓑ Ⓒ Ⓓ Ⓔ
28. Ⓐ Ⓑ Ⓒ Ⓓ Ⓔ
29. Ⓐ Ⓑ Ⓒ Ⓓ Ⓔ
30. Ⓐ Ⓑ Ⓒ Ⓓ Ⓔ
31. Ⓐ Ⓑ Ⓒ Ⓓ Ⓔ
32. Ⓐ Ⓑ Ⓒ Ⓓ Ⓔ
33. Ⓐ Ⓑ Ⓒ Ⓓ Ⓔ

34. Ⓐ Ⓑ Ⓒ Ⓓ Ⓔ
35. Ⓐ Ⓑ Ⓒ Ⓓ Ⓔ
36. Ⓐ Ⓑ Ⓒ Ⓓ Ⓔ
37. Ⓐ Ⓑ Ⓒ Ⓓ Ⓔ
38. Ⓐ Ⓑ Ⓒ Ⓓ Ⓔ
39. Ⓐ Ⓑ Ⓒ Ⓓ Ⓔ
40. Ⓐ Ⓑ Ⓒ Ⓓ Ⓔ
41. Ⓐ Ⓑ Ⓒ Ⓓ Ⓔ
42. Ⓐ Ⓑ Ⓒ Ⓓ Ⓔ
43. Ⓐ Ⓑ Ⓒ Ⓓ Ⓔ
44. Ⓐ Ⓑ Ⓒ Ⓓ Ⓔ
45. Ⓐ Ⓑ Ⓒ Ⓓ Ⓔ
46. Ⓐ Ⓑ Ⓒ Ⓓ Ⓔ
47. Ⓐ Ⓑ Ⓒ Ⓓ Ⓔ
48. Ⓐ Ⓑ Ⓒ Ⓓ Ⓔ
49. Ⓐ Ⓑ Ⓒ Ⓓ Ⓔ
50. Ⓐ Ⓑ Ⓒ Ⓓ Ⓔ
51. Ⓐ Ⓑ Ⓒ Ⓓ Ⓔ
52. Ⓐ Ⓑ Ⓒ Ⓓ Ⓔ
53. Ⓐ Ⓑ Ⓒ Ⓓ Ⓔ
54. Ⓐ Ⓑ Ⓒ Ⓓ Ⓔ
55. Ⓐ Ⓑ Ⓒ Ⓓ Ⓔ
56. Ⓐ Ⓑ Ⓒ Ⓓ Ⓔ
57. Ⓐ Ⓑ Ⓒ Ⓓ Ⓔ
58. Ⓐ Ⓑ Ⓒ Ⓓ Ⓔ
59. Ⓐ Ⓑ Ⓒ Ⓓ Ⓔ
60. Ⓐ Ⓑ Ⓒ Ⓓ Ⓔ
61. Ⓐ Ⓑ Ⓒ Ⓓ Ⓔ
62. Ⓐ Ⓑ Ⓒ Ⓓ Ⓔ
63. Ⓐ Ⓑ Ⓒ Ⓓ Ⓔ
64. Ⓐ Ⓑ Ⓒ Ⓓ Ⓔ
65. Ⓐ Ⓑ Ⓒ Ⓓ Ⓔ
66. Ⓐ Ⓑ Ⓒ Ⓓ Ⓔ

67. Ⓐ Ⓑ Ⓒ Ⓓ Ⓔ
68. Ⓐ Ⓑ Ⓒ Ⓓ Ⓔ
69. Ⓐ Ⓑ Ⓒ Ⓓ Ⓔ
70. Ⓐ Ⓑ Ⓒ Ⓓ Ⓔ
71. Ⓐ Ⓑ Ⓒ Ⓓ Ⓔ
72. Ⓐ Ⓑ Ⓒ Ⓓ Ⓔ
73. Ⓐ Ⓑ Ⓒ Ⓓ Ⓔ
74. Ⓐ Ⓑ Ⓒ Ⓓ Ⓔ
75. Ⓐ Ⓑ Ⓒ Ⓓ Ⓔ
76. Ⓐ Ⓑ Ⓒ Ⓓ Ⓔ
77. Ⓐ Ⓑ Ⓒ Ⓓ Ⓔ
78. Ⓐ Ⓑ Ⓒ Ⓓ Ⓔ
79. Ⓐ Ⓑ Ⓒ Ⓓ Ⓔ
80. Ⓐ Ⓑ Ⓒ Ⓓ Ⓔ
81. Ⓐ Ⓑ Ⓒ Ⓓ Ⓔ
82. Ⓐ Ⓑ Ⓒ Ⓓ Ⓔ
83. Ⓐ Ⓑ Ⓒ Ⓓ Ⓔ
84. Ⓐ Ⓑ Ⓒ Ⓓ Ⓔ
85. Ⓐ Ⓑ Ⓒ Ⓓ Ⓔ
86. Ⓐ Ⓑ Ⓒ Ⓓ Ⓔ
87. Ⓐ Ⓑ Ⓒ Ⓓ Ⓔ
88. Ⓐ Ⓑ Ⓒ Ⓓ Ⓔ
89. Ⓐ Ⓑ Ⓒ Ⓓ Ⓔ
90. Ⓐ Ⓑ Ⓒ Ⓓ Ⓔ
91. Ⓐ Ⓑ Ⓒ Ⓓ Ⓔ
92. Ⓐ Ⓑ Ⓒ Ⓓ Ⓔ
93. Ⓐ Ⓑ Ⓒ Ⓓ Ⓔ
94. Ⓐ Ⓑ Ⓒ Ⓓ Ⓔ
95. Ⓐ Ⓑ Ⓒ Ⓓ Ⓔ
96. Ⓐ Ⓑ Ⓒ Ⓓ Ⓔ
97. Ⓐ Ⓑ Ⓒ Ⓓ Ⓔ
98. Ⓐ Ⓑ Ⓒ Ⓓ Ⓔ
99. Ⓐ Ⓑ Ⓒ Ⓓ Ⓔ
100. Ⓐ Ⓑ Ⓒ Ⓓ Ⓔ

PRACTICE TEST 2

Answer Sheet

1. Ⓐ Ⓑ Ⓒ Ⓓ Ⓔ	34. Ⓐ Ⓑ Ⓒ Ⓓ Ⓔ	67. Ⓐ Ⓑ Ⓒ Ⓓ Ⓔ
2. Ⓐ Ⓑ Ⓒ Ⓓ Ⓔ	35. Ⓐ Ⓑ Ⓒ Ⓓ Ⓔ	68. Ⓐ Ⓑ Ⓒ Ⓓ Ⓔ
3. Ⓐ Ⓑ Ⓒ Ⓓ Ⓔ	36. Ⓐ Ⓑ Ⓒ Ⓓ Ⓔ	69. Ⓐ Ⓑ Ⓒ Ⓓ Ⓔ
4. Ⓐ Ⓑ Ⓒ Ⓓ Ⓔ	37. Ⓐ Ⓑ Ⓒ Ⓓ Ⓔ	70. Ⓐ Ⓑ Ⓒ Ⓓ Ⓔ
5. Ⓐ Ⓑ Ⓒ Ⓓ Ⓔ	38. Ⓐ Ⓑ Ⓒ Ⓓ Ⓔ	71. Ⓐ Ⓑ Ⓒ Ⓓ Ⓔ
6. Ⓐ Ⓑ Ⓒ Ⓓ Ⓔ	39. Ⓐ Ⓑ Ⓒ Ⓓ Ⓔ	72. Ⓐ Ⓑ Ⓒ Ⓓ Ⓔ
7. Ⓐ Ⓑ Ⓒ Ⓓ Ⓔ	40. Ⓐ Ⓑ Ⓒ Ⓓ Ⓔ	73. Ⓐ Ⓑ Ⓒ Ⓓ Ⓔ
8. Ⓐ Ⓑ Ⓒ Ⓓ Ⓔ	41. Ⓐ Ⓑ Ⓒ Ⓓ Ⓔ	74. Ⓐ Ⓑ Ⓒ Ⓓ Ⓔ
9. Ⓐ Ⓑ Ⓒ Ⓓ Ⓔ	42. Ⓐ Ⓑ Ⓒ Ⓓ Ⓔ	75. Ⓐ Ⓑ Ⓒ Ⓓ Ⓔ
10. Ⓐ Ⓑ Ⓒ Ⓓ Ⓔ	43. Ⓐ Ⓑ Ⓒ Ⓓ Ⓔ	76. Ⓐ Ⓑ Ⓒ Ⓓ Ⓔ
11. Ⓐ Ⓑ Ⓒ Ⓓ Ⓔ	44. Ⓐ Ⓑ Ⓒ Ⓓ Ⓔ	77. Ⓐ Ⓑ Ⓒ Ⓓ Ⓔ
12. Ⓐ Ⓑ Ⓒ Ⓓ Ⓔ	45. Ⓐ Ⓑ Ⓒ Ⓓ Ⓔ	78. Ⓐ Ⓑ Ⓒ Ⓓ Ⓔ
13. Ⓐ Ⓑ Ⓒ Ⓓ Ⓔ	46. Ⓐ Ⓑ Ⓒ Ⓓ Ⓔ	79. Ⓐ Ⓑ Ⓒ Ⓓ Ⓔ
14. Ⓐ Ⓑ Ⓒ Ⓓ Ⓔ	47. Ⓐ Ⓑ Ⓒ Ⓓ Ⓔ	80. Ⓐ Ⓑ Ⓒ Ⓓ Ⓔ
15. Ⓐ Ⓑ Ⓒ Ⓓ Ⓔ	48. Ⓐ Ⓑ Ⓒ Ⓓ Ⓔ	81. Ⓐ Ⓑ Ⓒ Ⓓ Ⓔ
16. Ⓐ Ⓑ Ⓒ Ⓓ Ⓔ	49. Ⓐ Ⓑ Ⓒ Ⓓ Ⓔ	82. Ⓐ Ⓑ Ⓒ Ⓓ Ⓔ
17. Ⓐ Ⓑ Ⓒ Ⓓ Ⓔ	50. Ⓐ Ⓑ Ⓒ Ⓓ Ⓔ	83. Ⓐ Ⓑ Ⓒ Ⓓ Ⓔ
18. Ⓐ Ⓑ Ⓒ Ⓓ Ⓔ	51. Ⓐ Ⓑ Ⓒ Ⓓ Ⓔ	84. Ⓐ Ⓑ Ⓒ Ⓓ Ⓔ
19. Ⓐ Ⓑ Ⓒ Ⓓ Ⓔ	52. Ⓐ Ⓑ Ⓒ Ⓓ Ⓔ	85. Ⓐ Ⓑ Ⓒ Ⓓ Ⓔ
20. Ⓐ Ⓑ Ⓒ Ⓓ Ⓔ	53. Ⓐ Ⓑ Ⓒ Ⓓ Ⓔ	86. Ⓐ Ⓑ Ⓒ Ⓓ Ⓔ
21. Ⓐ Ⓑ Ⓒ Ⓓ Ⓔ	54. Ⓐ Ⓑ Ⓒ Ⓓ Ⓔ	87. Ⓐ Ⓑ Ⓒ Ⓓ Ⓔ
22. Ⓐ Ⓑ Ⓒ Ⓓ Ⓔ	55. Ⓐ Ⓑ Ⓒ Ⓓ Ⓔ	88. Ⓐ Ⓑ Ⓒ Ⓓ Ⓔ
23. Ⓐ Ⓑ Ⓒ Ⓓ Ⓔ	56. Ⓐ Ⓑ Ⓒ Ⓓ Ⓔ	89. Ⓐ Ⓑ Ⓒ Ⓓ Ⓔ
24. Ⓐ Ⓑ Ⓒ Ⓓ Ⓔ	57. Ⓐ Ⓑ Ⓒ Ⓓ Ⓔ	90. Ⓐ Ⓑ Ⓒ Ⓓ Ⓔ
25. Ⓐ Ⓑ Ⓒ Ⓓ Ⓔ	58. Ⓐ Ⓑ Ⓒ Ⓓ Ⓔ	91. Ⓐ Ⓑ Ⓒ Ⓓ Ⓔ
26. Ⓐ Ⓑ Ⓒ Ⓓ Ⓔ	59. Ⓐ Ⓑ Ⓒ Ⓓ Ⓔ	92. Ⓐ Ⓑ Ⓒ Ⓓ Ⓔ
27. Ⓐ Ⓑ Ⓒ Ⓓ Ⓔ	60. Ⓐ Ⓑ Ⓒ Ⓓ Ⓔ	93. Ⓐ Ⓑ Ⓒ Ⓓ Ⓔ
28. Ⓐ Ⓑ Ⓒ Ⓓ Ⓔ	61. Ⓐ Ⓑ Ⓒ Ⓓ Ⓔ	94. Ⓐ Ⓑ Ⓒ Ⓓ Ⓔ
29. Ⓐ Ⓑ Ⓒ Ⓓ Ⓔ	62. Ⓐ Ⓑ Ⓒ Ⓓ Ⓔ	95. Ⓐ Ⓑ Ⓒ Ⓓ Ⓔ
30. Ⓐ Ⓑ Ⓒ Ⓓ Ⓔ	63. Ⓐ Ⓑ Ⓒ Ⓓ Ⓔ	96. Ⓐ Ⓑ Ⓒ Ⓓ Ⓔ
31. Ⓐ Ⓑ Ⓒ Ⓓ Ⓔ	64. Ⓐ Ⓑ Ⓒ Ⓓ Ⓔ	97. Ⓐ Ⓑ Ⓒ Ⓓ Ⓔ
32. Ⓐ Ⓑ Ⓒ Ⓓ Ⓔ	65. Ⓐ Ⓑ Ⓒ Ⓓ Ⓔ	98. Ⓐ Ⓑ Ⓒ Ⓓ Ⓔ
33. Ⓐ Ⓑ Ⓒ Ⓓ Ⓔ	66. Ⓐ Ⓑ Ⓒ Ⓓ Ⓔ	99. Ⓐ Ⓑ Ⓒ Ⓓ Ⓔ
		100. Ⓐ Ⓑ Ⓒ Ⓓ Ⓔ

Glossary

accessory equipment: Capital goods used in the production process (e.g., assembly line equipment, drill presses, lathes).

accumulation: The process of assembling and pooling relatively small individual shipments so that they can be transported more economically.

administered: Arrangements that coordinate channel operations through a dominant channel member.

advertising budget: The determination of a specific dollar allocation; reflects the costs associated with alternative media and production costs.

advertising effectiveness: Assessed by both direct (sales, store traffic, coupon redemption rates) and indirect (consumers' recall of ads) measures.

agents: Independent wholesalers that do not take title of the products that they handle.

all available funds: Technique that allocates remaining resources to promotional activities.

allowances: Price reductions that are intended to achieve specific goals.

alternative pricing objectives: A firm's pricing strategy may reflect short-term goals other than profit maximization.

approach: Seller first meets the prospective buyer; goal at this stage is to gain the interest and attention of the buyer.

assorting: The process of acquiring a wide variety of merchandise to meet the diverse preferences of consumers.

atmosphere: Those characteristics that contribute to consumers' general impression of the store—its image.

behavioral dimensions: Include purchase occasion, user status, user rate, and brand loyalty as well as customer attitudes toward products and product benefits.

Boston Consulting Group matrix: Framework that classifies each product or product line within a firm's "product portfolio."

brainstorming: Small-group technique that encourages participants to voice creative ideas on a specified topic.

break-even analysis: Allows managers to estimate the impact of alternative price levels on profits.

brokers: Temporary wholesalers.

business analysis: Detailed evaluation of a concept's commercial feasibility.

buyers: Individuals who identify suppliers, arrange terms of sale, and carry out purchasing procedures.

buying center: Entity comprised of all the people who participate in or influence the decision-making process.

buying situation: Can be characterized as one of three types—new-task buying, straight rebuy, or modified rebuy.

buying-related behaviors: Seeking out product information or shopping to compare alternative brands, stores, and prices.

canned: Sales presentations that are memorized messages.

cash cows: Generate large profits and require relatively little investment to maintain their market share in slow-growth industries.

cash discounts: Given to encourage buyers to provide payment promptly.

channel conflict: When disagreements arise between members over channel practices and policies.

channel control: The ability to influence the actions of other channel members.

channel length: The number of levels used to create a distribution channel.

channel width: The number of independent members at one level of the distribution channel (e.g., producer, wholesaler, retailer, final consumer).

closing the sale: Stage at which the seller tries to gain a purchase commitment from the prospect.

codes of conduct: Intended to eliminate opportunities for unethical behavior that will reflect badly on an organization.

cognitive dissonance: State of mental anxiety that can be caused by a consumer's uncertainty about a purchase.

commercialization: Marks the start of full-scale production and the implementation of the complete marketing plan.

communication channels: Medium through which promotional messages are sent and delivered.

compensatory: Ethical models where the moral right or wrong of an action is determined by the consequences the action produces.

competition-based pricing: Prices set according to those charged by a firm's closest competitors.

competitive parity: Approach establishes a budget based on the actions of a firm's closest competitors.

component materials: Used in the production of finished goods.

concept testing: Subjects new ideas to consumer scrutiny.

consumer goods: Classified as one of three product types—convenience, shopping, and specialty.

consumer products: Products targeted toward individuals and households for final consumption.

consumer-directed: Promotional tools that include coupons, contests, sweepstakes, rebates, premiums, refunds, etc.

containerization: The process of consolidating many items into one container.

contractual: Arrangements that specify performance terms for each independent channel member.

convenience goods: Goods purchased frequently and with a minimum of shopping effort (low-involvement decision-making).

corporate: Channel of distribution where one firm owns either all channel members or firms at the next level in the channel.

corporate chains: Several (usually 10 or more) stores that are owned and managed by the same firm.

cost-based pricing: Establishes product prices as a function of product costs.

cost-per-thousand: Advertising costs evaluated according to the cost of reaching a thousand prospects through a given vehicle.

creative platform: Provides the overall concept and theme for an advertising campaign.

customary prices: Attempt to combat rising costs by reducing the size of each package or changing the ingredients used in production.

customer service standard: Different customers requiring different levels of service.

customer size: Based on the purchasing power of buyers rather than the number of buyers.

customer type: Includes manufacturers, wholesalers, retailers, government agencies, and nonprofit institutions.

databases: Contain information about prior purchase behavior, demographics, psychographics, and geographic data.

dealer brands: Brands created by intermediaries (e.g., retailers); also known as private brands.

deciders: The individual(s) who makes the final purchase decision.

deep product mixes: Focuses a firm's resources on a smaller number of product lines which, in turn, allows the development of several products within each line.

demand-based pricing: Sets prices based on consumer responses to product prices.

derived demand: Organizational buyers derive their demand for materials from the anticipated demand by consumers for finished goods.

differential advantage: The unique qualities of a product that encourage customer purchase and loyalty.

diffusion process: The typical rate of adoption exhibited by consumers in response to new products; there are five categories of adopters—innovators, early adopters, early majority, late majority, and laggards.

direct channels: Channel systems that move goods from the producer to the final consumer without using independent intermediaries or "middlemen."

direct marketing: One-on-one communications with targeted customers; aimed primarily at obtaining an immediate response.

discounts: Reductions from list prices that are given by sellers to buyers.

distribution centers: Type of warehouse planned in relation to specific markets.

distribution-center concept: The most effective strategy may be a compromise between two extremes.

diversification strategy: Aims new products at new markets.

dogs: Characterized by low profitability and little opportunity for sales growth.

drawing account method: Sales commissions are credited to each individual's drawing account.

drop shippers: Limited-service merchant wholesalers that buy products from manufacturers and arrange for the delivery to retailers.

economic order quantity (EOQ): The order size that minimizes the total cost of ordering and carrying inventory.

elastic demand: Increase in price will produce a decrease in demand and a decrease in total revenue; conversely, price decreases will increase demand and increase total revenue.

electronic commerce: All forms of buying and selling that are supported by electronic means.

electronic data interchange (EDI): Allows a company to integrate order processing, production, inventory planning, and transportation into a single system.

evaluation process: Comparisons such as sales/sales potential and sales expense/sales that are made to the same salesperson's performance in previous periods or to the performance standards established by others.

exclusive distribution: Strategy that limits the number of outlets employed to one or two intermediaries within each market.

experimental research: Compares the impact of marketing variables on individuals' responses in a controlled setting.

extended product: Includes both the tangible and intangible elements (such as brand image and accompanying service features) of a product; also known as augmented product.

fabricated parts: Used in the production of finished goods.

family brand: Type of strategy in which the same brand is applied to several products.

focus group: In-person data collection procedure in which the interviewer meets with five to ten persons at the same time.

follow-up: Represents the salesperson's efforts to assure customer satisfaction after the sale.

forecasting: A highly specialized function of marketing information systems that estimates the demand for a brand or product category.

franchise systems: Specific type of vertical marketing system in which the parent company (franchisor) provides franchisees with the legal right to use company trademarks.

freight forwarders: Specialized agencies that provide alternate forms of transportation coordination.

frequency: Refers to the average number of times that members of the target audience are exposed to an ad through a given vehicle.

full-service merchant wholesalers: Perform the complete range of wholesaling functions.

gatekeepers: People within an organization who control the flow of relevant purchase-related information.

geographic demographics: Identifiable characteristics of towns, cities, states, regions, and countries; include county size, city or SMSA (Standard Metropolitan Statistical Area) size, population density, and climate.

geographic pricing: Policy that reflects different levels of transportation and other costs related to the physical distance between buyers and sellers.

green marketing: Design, development, and marketing of products that do not harm the environment.

gross rating points (GRPs): Calculated by multiplying reach times frequency.

guaranteed draw: Salesperson is not obligated to pay back the difference when the draw exceeds commissions earned over a specified period.

homogeneous: Potential buyers within each segment who are more similar to each other on key dimensions than to buyers assigned to other segments.

horizontal integration: The process of acquiring firms that operate at the same channel level.

idea generation: The process of searching for new product opportunities.

ideal points: Identify consumers' perception of the perfect bundle or combination of attributes.

independent stores: Single retail units that are not affiliated with a corporate chain or cooperative.

indirect channels: Channels that move goods with the cooperation and assistance of independent intermediaries.

individual brands: Brands assigned to each product when there exists significant variation in product type and quality.

industrial products: Products typically purchased for resale, operational needs, or use in further production; sometimes called business products.

inelastic demand: Increase in price will produce a decrease in demand and an increase in total revenue while price decreases will increase demand and decrease total revenue.

influencers: Individuals who establish product requirements and specifications based on their technical expertise or authority within an organization.

information: Function of packaging that permits consumers to critically evaluate products and compare brands.

inseparability: A service cannot be separated from the person providing it.

installations: Capital goods used in the production process (e.g., assembly line equipment, drill presses, lathes).

intangible: The fact that something is not actually experienced by buyers until the service is performed.

integrated marketing communications (ICM): Planning a comprehensive program that coordinates all promotional activities.

intensive distribution: Strategy in which a firm sells through every potential outlet that will reach its target market.

interactive: Presentations that rely heavily on learning more about each prospect's needs and preferences through direct interaction.

intermediary-directed: Promotional activities ranging from push money, trade allowances, and quantity discounts to sales contests, trade shows, point-of-purchase display materials, and trade rebates.

intermodal transportation: Two or more transportation modes used in combination.

involvement: The importance that consumers attach to the purchase of a particular product.

just-in-time (JIT): Making products and materials available just as needed for production or resale.

leader pricing: Occurs when a firm sells select products below their usual price as a means of gaining attention or building store traffic.

licensed brand: A well-established brand name that other sellers pay to use.

limited-service merchant wholesalers: May not provide merchandising or market research assistance.

long-term forecasts: Typically done for a five-year period and play a significant role in strategic planning.

macroenvironmental factors: External forces that impact all firms within an industry; includes demographics or demography, economic conditions, competition, social and cultural factors, political and legal factors (government), and technological factors.

manufacturer brands: Brands created by product manufacturers; sometimes called national brands.

manufacturer wholesaling: When the product's producer performs the wholesaling functions.

markdowns: Retail price reductions.

market: People or organizations that want or need a product and have the willingness and ability to buy.

market development strategy: Attempts to increase sales by introducing existing products to new markets.

market penetration strategy: Attempts to increase sales of a firm's existing products to its current markets.

market segmentation: The process of dividing the total market into distinct submarkets or groups based on similarities in their wants, needs, behaviors, or other characteristics.

market segments: Groups of customers who are similar to each other in a meaningful way and who will respond to a firm's marketing mix similarly.

market targeting: Once the segmentation process is complete, each resulting segment is evaluated in terms of its attractiveness for a firm, and a firm's target market(s) is chosen based on this evaluation.

marketing: The process of planning and executing the development, pricing, promotion, and distribution of goods and services to achieve organizational goals.

marketing concept: Customer-oriented business philosophy that stresses customer satisfaction as the key to achieving organizational goals.

marketing environment: Composed of two types of factors—those that an organization can control and those that it cannot control.

marketing ethics: Moral principles that define right and wrong behavior in marketing practice.

marketing functions: Consist of environmental analysis, consumer analysis, product planning, price planning, promotion planning, and physical distribution (place) planning.

marketing information system (MIS): The people, equipment, and procedures used to gather, sort, analyze, evaluate, and distribute accurate information to marketing decision makers.

marketing mix: Combination of four variables (product, price, promotion, and physical distribution) that comprise an organization's marketing program.

marketing myopia: Term used to characterize short-sighted marketing strategy.

marketing objectives: The goals of a firm in both quantitative (e.g., sales, profit, market share) and qualitative (e.g., market leadership, corporate image) terms.

marketing plan: An organization's statement of marketing strategy and the specification of the activities required to carry out the strategy.

marketing plan development: Focuses on how the elements of the marketing mix can be most effectively used.

marketing research: The systematic process of planning, collecting, analyzing, and communicating information that is relevant to making better marketing decisions.

marketing research process: Designed to yield reliable and objective answers to specific marketing questions; can be described in six distinct steps.

marketing strategy: Defines the way in which the marketing mix is used to satisfy the needs of the target market and to achieve organizational goals.

markups: Percentages or dollar amounts added to the cost of sales to arrive at the product's selling price.

materials handling: The physical handling of goods in both warehouse and transportation functions.

media planning: The choice of media-type and the selection of specific vehicles within each medium.

medium-term forecasts: Typically done annually and provide input to annual marketing plan review and revision.

meeting objections: May represent a request for clarification or additional information.

megacarriers: Freight transport companies that provide several shipment modes.

merchant wholesalers: Independent firms that take title and possession of the products they sell; sometimes referred to as distributors or jobbers.

microenvironmental factors: External forces that impact each specific company uniquely, such as suppliers, marketing intermediaries, and the target market.

mix expansion: Provides a firm with new opportunities for growth.

modified rebuy: Process used when the purchase situation is less complex than new-task buying and more involved than a straight rebuy; some information is required to reach decisions and a limited number of alternatives may be evaluated.

monitoring the performance: Requires the collection of either qualitative or quantitative information.

multiple channels: When a firm develops two or more separate and distinct distribution channels; also called dual distribution.

multiple segmentation strategy: The choice to pursue more than one target market with corresponding marketing mixes for each; also known as differentiated marketing.

multi-variable segmentation: Recognizes the importance of interrelationships between factors in defining market segments, such as age, income, and education.

new product opportunities: Can stem from the modification of existing products or the development of wholly new product innovations.

new-task buying: The most complex of the three buy classes; requires greater effort in gathering information and evaluating alternatives; frequently employed in the purchase of high-cost products.

noncompensatory: Ethical models that maintain a universally true moral principle with no exceptions.

non-probability samples: Nonrandom samples.

non-store retailing: Retail transactions that occur outside of traditional store settings; two-way interaction between a marketer and individual consumers to both obtain an immediate response and cultivate lasting customer relationships; also known as direct marketing.

objective and task: Procedure relies on the matching of promotional objectives to the funding required to achieve specific, objective-related tasks.

objectives: Determined by the marketing strategy for the product or firm.

observation: An unobtrusive data collection procedure in which subjects' behaviors are observed without their knowledge.

odd-even pricing: Sets prices just below even dollar values (e.g., $99.99 or $99 v. $100).

one-price: Policy that offers the same price to all buyers for purchases of essentially the same quantities in comparable situations.

online marketing: All marketing activities conducted through interactive online computer networks or systems that link buyers and sellers.

operating supplies: Low-cost items that aid in the production process (e.g., lubricating oils, pencils, janitorial supplies).

opportunities: Favorable environmental conditions that could bring a firm rewards if exploited.

order getters: Responsible for securing new business for a firm.

order leadtime: The average length of time between the customer placing an order and receiving it.

order processing: The receipt and transmission of sales order information.

order takers: Service customer accounts that have already been established.

ownership: Classification method for retailers.

partnership selling: Formal arrangements between buyers and sellers that create unique, customized products and services for the buyer.

penetration pricing: Alternative pricing strategy for new product introductions that uses low introductory prices to gain a large share of the market more quickly than price skimming would allow.

percent-of-sales: Allocates a fixed percentage of the previous year's sales for promotional programs.

perishable: Notion that services cannot be inventoried, returned, or resold.

personal demographics: Identifiable characteristics of individuals and groups of people; variables include age, sex, family size, income, occupation, and education.

pre-approach: Salesperson must decide how to best initiate a face-to-face meeting.

presentation: Message is intended to persuade buyers to purchase based on the attributes and benefits of the seller's product.

prestige pricing: Establishes retail prices that are high, relative to competing brands; intended to suggest higher product quality.

price elasticity of demand coefficient (E_d): Equal to the absolute value or non-negative value of the price elasticity of demand formula.

price lining: Simplifies consumers' evaluation of alternative products by establishing a limited number of price points for groups or lines of products.

price skimming: Strategy that introduces new products at relatively high prices.

primary data: Information collected specifically for the current research study.

probability samples: persons selected at random from the designated population.

problem child: Does not provide great profits but still requires high levels of investment to maintain or increase market share.

product: Good, service, idea, place, or person.

product adoption: When the buyer decides to continue using a product regularly.

product adoption process: The stages that consumers go through in learning about new products.

product development: Stage in which viable ideas are first produced in tangible form and the initial marketing strategy is created.

product development strategy: Entails offering new products to a firm's current markets.

product differentiation: When a product or brand is perceived as different from its competitors on any tangible or intangible characteristic.

product line: Consists of a group or set of closely related items that usually share some common attributes.

product mix: Comprised of all the product lines that a firm offers.

product positioning: The process of developing a product or brand image in the consumer's mind.

product screening: Potential products sorted relative to their strengths and weaknesses.

product/market opportunity matrix: Specifies four fundamental alternative marketing strategies available to a firm—market penetration, market development, product development, and diversification.

promotion: Function of packaging that represents the last opportunity to influence decision making.

promotion mix: Elements that contribute to a firm's overall communications program; includes advertising, personal selling, publicity, public relations, and sales promotions.

promotion objectives: Address three goals (inform, persuade, remind) within the marketing mix.

prospecting: The process of seeking and identifying prospective buyers or "leads."

protection: Function of packaging that can prevent product damage and spoilage.

psychographics: Factors that influence consumers' patterns of living or lifestyle, such as activities, interests, opinions (AIOs) as well as social class, personality, and values.

pulling: Generating consumer demand for the product as a means of securing support within the channel.

pushing: Utilizing promotional efforts to secure the cooperation of intermediaries.

qualifying leads: Salesperson determines whether the prospect is both willing and able to buy.

quantity discounts: Arise from the economies and improved efficiency of selling in large quantities.

rack jobbers: Full-service merchant wholesalers that provide the display racks used to merchandise the product.

raw materials: Used in the production of finished goods.

reach: Percentage of a target audience that is exposed to an ad through a given vehicle, within a specified time frame.

relationship selling: Salesperson's activities that are focused on building ties to the customer.

reorder point: The inventory level at which new orders need to be placed to avoid a stockout.

research design: Specifies the plan for collecting and analyzing data.

retail store location: A function of the target market, location of competitors, and site costs.

retailing: All the activities related to the sale of products to final consumers for individual or household consumption.

reverse logistics: Concept that emphasizes the responsibility of a firm for products after they are disposed of by consumers.

Robinson-Patman Act: Prohibits any form of price discrimination that has the effect of reducing competition among wholesalers or retailers.

safety stock: The amount of extra inventory kept on hand to avoid stockouts.

sales force allocation: An attempt to match the talent and ability of salespeople to the characteristics of the customers within the territory.

sales force structure: How sellers choose to organize their sales force.

sales potential: The maximum possible sales within a territory.

sales promotion: All paid marketing communications other than advertising, public relations, and personal selling.

salesforce compensation: May take one of three basic forms—straight salary, straight commission, or a combination plan.

sample size: Larger sample sizes yield more reliable results but are also more expensive than smaller samples.

sampling: The process of gathering data from a selected subgroup (sample) chosen from the population of interest.

scrambled merchandising: Takes place as retailers add products that are not related to their traditional lines.

seasonal discounts: Used to encourage buyers to make their purchases off-season.

secondary data: Information that has already been collected for reasons not directly related to the current study.

segmenting: Two-step process in which variables are first chosen and then the market is divided along those dimensions followed by profiling of the resulting segments.

selective distribution: Strategy in which a firm sells through many, but not all, potential wholesalers and retailers.

selling process: Sequence of stages that are essential to effective personal selling.

service marketing: Marketing geared toward something other than manufactured goods.

services: Tasks performed by one individual or firm for another; may be classified as either consumer services or industrial services, depending on the customers served.

Sherman Act: Prevents businesses from restraining trade and interstate commerce.

shopping goods: Goods for which consumers typically make price-quality comparisons at several stores before buying (high-involvement decision-making).

short-term forecasts: Typically predict sales for the next month or quarter and are used for production scheduling and evaluating the impact of short-term promotions.

simulation: Technique that utilizes computer-based programs to assess the impact of alternative marketing strategies.

single-segment strategy: The decision to focus on one segment as a target market; also known as concentration strategy.

single-variable segmentation: Characterized by one segmentation variable.

situation analysis: Examines economic environment; technological developments; social changes, changes in buying behavior; legal and political developments; size of the existing market and the potential market; rate of market growth; buyer behavior; brand loyalty; competitive behavior, and market share trends; identifies a company's relative strengths and weaknesses, as well as the opportunities and threats posed by its marketing environment.

social responsibility: A firm's obligations to society that is comprised of four dimensions—economic, legal, ethical, and philanthropic.

sorting: The process of separating goods by quality, color, or size.

specialty goods: Goods for which buyers have strong brand loyalty; they'll accept no substitutes.

stars: Generate large profits but also consume substantial resources to finance their continued growth.

stockout: A shortage of product resulting from carrying too few in inventory.

straight rebuy: Process used to purchase inexpensive, low-risk products; in most instances, previous purchases are simply reordered to replace depleted inventory; alternative products or suppliers are not typically considered or evaluated.

strategy development: Questions addressed by marketing research, such as: What business should we be in? How will we compete? What are the goals for the business?

strengths: Competitive advantages or distinctive competencies that give a firm a superior ability to meet the needs of its target markets.

suboptimization: Cost-reducing actions in one distribution function that increase the overall cost of other distribution functions.

support salespeople: Provide assistance to both the order getters and order takers.

survey research: Means of systematically acquiring information from individuals by communicating directly with them.

sustainable competitive advantage: An enduring differential advantage held over competitors by offering buyers superior value either through lower prices or other elements of the marketing mix.

SWOT matrix: Tool used to assess the potential value and fit of new opportunities.

tangible product: Consists of those features that can be precisely specified (e.g., color, size, weight).

target market: A particular group of potential customers that an organization seeks to satisfy with a product.

test marketing: Provides a series of commercial experiments to test the acceptance of a product and the appropriateness of the proposed marketing strategy.

threats: Competitive conditions or other barriers that might prevent a firm from reaching its goals.

total-cost concept: Minimizing costs and satisfying customer demands, which can represent conflicting objectives.

trade discounts: Reductions from the list price given to intermediaries in exchange for the performance of specified tasks.

trademarks: Brand names, marks, or characters used to identify products.

transportation modes: The means of moving goods from one location to another; five major modes are railroads, trucks, waterways, airways, and pipelines.

types of warehouses: Includes private and public warehouses, distribution centers, and bonded storage.

undifferentiated marketing: Treating the total potential market as a whole—one vast target market; also known as mass marketing.

unit loading: The grouping of boxes on a pallet or skid.

unit pricing: Provides consumers with information on the price per unit on or near the product.

unitary elasticity: Total revenue does not change in response to price increases or decreases.

unsought goods: Goods for which no demand exists.

usage rate: The rate at which inventory is sold per time period.

users: People within a firm who will use the product.

variable: Services are not performed in the same way each and every time.

vertical integration: The process of acquiring firms that operate at different channel levels.

vertical marketing systems: A collective means of enhancing the market power of individually owned retail units.

warehousing: The process of designing and operating facilities for both storing and moving goods.

weaknesses: Limitations that a company might face in the development or implementation of a specific marketing strategy.

wheel of retailing: Theory that new retailers enter markets as low-status, low-price competitors; if successful, they tend to evolve into more traditional forms, adding customer-service features and raising prices to meet higher operating costs, which allows new retailers to enter the market.

wholesaling: All the activities related to the resale of products to organizational buyers, other wholesalers, and retailers; typically include warehousing, transporting, and financing.

wide product mix: A diversification strategy that offers several different product lines that enable a firm to meet several different types of customer needs.

Index

Notes

Notes

Notes

Notes

Notes

Notes

Notes

Notes

Notes

Notes

REA's Test Preps

The Best in Test Preparation

- REA "Test Preps" are **far more** comprehensive than any other test preparation series
- Each book contains full-length practice tests based on the most recent exams
- **Every** type of question likely to be given on the exams is included
- Answers are accompanied by **full** and **detailed** explanations

REA publishes hundreds of test prep books. Some of our titles include:

Advanced Placement Exams (APs)
Art History
Biology
Calculus AB & BC
Chemistry
Economics
English Language &
    Composition
English Literature &
    Composition
European History
French Language
Government & Politics
Latin Vergil
Physics B & C
Psychology
Spanish Language
Statistics
United States History
World History

**College-Level Examination
    Program (CLEP)**
American Government
College Algebra
General Examinations
History of the United States I
History of the United States II
Introduction to Educational
    Psychology
Human Growth and Development
Introductory Psychology
Introductory Sociology
Principles of Management
Principles of Marketing
Spanish
Western Civilization I
Western Civilization II

SAT Subject Tests
Biology E/M
Chemistry
French
German
Literature
Mathematics Level 1, 2
Physics
Spanish
United States History

Graduate Record Exams (GREs)
Biology
Chemistry
General
Literature in English
Mathematics
Physics
Psychology

ACT - ACT Assessment

ASVAB - Armed Services
    Vocational Aptitude Battery

CBEST - California Basic Educational Skills Test

CDL - Commercial Driver License
    Exam

COOP, HSPT & TACHS - Catholic High
    School Admission Tests

FE (EIT) - AM Exam

FTCE - Florida Teacher Certification
    Examinations

GED

GMAT - Graduate Management
    Admission Test

LSAT - Law School Admission Test

MAT - Miller Analogies Test

MCAT - Medical College Admission
    Test

MTEL - Massachusetts Tests for
Educator Licensure

NJ HSPA - New Jersey High School
    Proficiency Assessment

NYSTCE - New York State Teacher
    Certification Examinations

PRAXIS PLT - Principles of
    Learning & Teaching Tests

PRAXIS PPST - Pre-Professional
Skills Tests

PSAT/NMSQT

SAT

TExES - Texas Examinations of
    Educator Standards

THEA - Texas Higher Education
    Assessment

TOEFL - Test of English as a
Foreign Language

USMLE Steps 1, 2 - U.S. Medical
    Licensing Exams

*For information about any of REA's
books, visit www.rea.com*

Research & Education Association
61 Ethel Road W., Piscataway, NJ 08854
Phone: (732) 819-8880